CONSUMER BEHAVIOR

George H. Haines, Jr.

CONSUMER
BEHAVIOR

LEARNING
MODELS
OF PURCHASING

Fp The Free Press, New York

Collier-Macmillan Limited, London

Copyright © 1969 by The Free Press

Collier-Macmillan Canada, Ltd., Toronto, Ontario

Library of Congress Catalog Card Number: 69-11164

First Printing

Printed in the United States of America

Apology

It is appropriate that this book should begin with an apology and not a preface for two reasons. First, this book could not have been written without the prior contributions of others; and second, it is the purpose of the book to present a theory of consumer behavior which at first glance will appear to dispense with long-standing constructs of economic theory (beginning with ordinal utility functions and ending with demand curves) that are well integrated into the main body of economic theory. The reason for proposing such an abrupt departure is simple. The theory presented in this book is designed to explain a class of behavior not explained by traditional economic theory. This class of behavior is clearly defined, and an effort made to present an orderly theory about it, in the chapters that follow. At the end, it must be noted, the argument will be presented that there may very well be no conflict between the theory of this book and what might be termed the traditional economic theory of consumer behavior.

The theory given here is not new. The first exploratory steps were taken by J. V. Yance, and the concepts were first formalized by A. A. Kuehn. Later writers have used or expanded upon Kuehn's original contribution in various directions; however, there existed no orderly presentation of this material. The present book was conceived as an effort to remedy this situation. In it, I have drawn heavily upon the works of these earlier authors, but the interpretation presented in this book is mine and mine alone. It is appropriate at this point to apologize to these authors (cited in the text) for any misconceptions or misuses of their works that may appear in the following pages.

The general outline of this book may be briefly described. The first chapter poses the problem and gives a short introduction to the type of solution proposed. This chapter, designed to discuss the essential points, omits some long derivations available elsewhere. It can be omitted by any reader uninterested in the rationale for the development of the "new" models of consumer behavior described in the rest of the book. The second chapter examines the behavioral assumptions underlying two basic classes of the "new" models of consumer behavior. This chapter suggests that the behavioral assumptions underlying the "new" models ought to be similar to those which have served economists so long and so well in the past.

The third chapter presents solutions to the aggregation problem posed in the second chapter. The fourth chapter discusses methods of subjecting the theory to test and presents some evidence to support the theoretical concepts previously developed. The last chapter discusses various issues that, despite their importance, were set aside as peripheral to the central argument at the time they were raised.

I should like to thank Harold H. Kassarjian, Donald Gordon, Harry L. Davis, Daniel Braunstein, Douglas Dalrymple, Leonard Simon, Marcus Alexis, James Ferguson, and Harry Gilman for helpful comments and also exonerate them from any remaining errors of omission or commission. A special debt is owed to Alvin J. G. Silk for his encouragement and innumerable helpful comments, which I hereby acknowledge. He too must be exonerated from any remaining errors. The members of two sessions of my course in marketing analysis, where the material in this book was classroom-tested, also contributed to whatever virtues this book has. I also acknowledge the great help given by Gary L. Grahn, who served as my research assistant while this manuscript was being prepared. Sandra Stephenson aided in preparing data for analysis. Finally, but certainly not last or least, Mrs. R. J. Messina and Mrs. Retta Holdorf must be thanked for their patient and expert secretarial assistance. Timely preparation of this manuscript was made possible not only by their efforts, but also by a research grant from the Executive Development Program of the University of Rochester.

GEORGE H. HAINES, JR.

Contents

Chapter 1

Preference Shifts and Consumer Behavior

Introduction

An allegation commonly made in the popular marketing literature, especially in basic marketing texts and occasionally in economic journals, is that economic theory is not capable of dealing with the fact that under certain conditions consumer preferences for goods may be variable.[1] Advertising, product promotions, and the introduction of new products are typically cited as phenomena that may cause shifts in consumer preferences. The fact that these allegations persist despite the existence of an apparently well-developed theory of demand with variable

---

1. See, for example, Dwight E. Robinson, "The Economics of Fashion Demand," *Quarterly Journal of Economics*, vol. LXXV, no. 3, August, 1961. The author is indebted to O. A. Davis, A. J. G. Silk, D. Gordon, and H. Davis for helpful comments on the material in this chapter. All remaining errors are the responsibility of the author, of course.

consumer preferences provides the beginning for this book and the substance of this chapter.

As is well known, the modern theory of consumer behavior is based on the assumption that the consumer allocates expenditures on commodities as if he had a fixed, ordered set of preferences, described by an indifference map or by an ordinal utility function, that he maximizes subject to constraints imposed by the income he receives and the prices he must pay. In a series of important papers, Ichimura, Tintner, and Basmann developed from this basis the existing theory of consumer behavior with variable preferences.[2]

This theory was developed in the hope that the analysis, entirely in terms of comparative statics, would provide a theoretical explanation of the way a hypothetical consumer, who always maximizes his utility function, reallocates a fixed total expenditure to purchases of goods and services when his preference structure is changed by an exogenous phenomenon— e.g., advertising—in certain defined ways. It was hoped that this theory would be as useful in the empirical analysis of the effects of advertising on demand as the theory of consumer demand with fixed preferences has been in empirical analysis of the effects of price and income on demand.

The first section of this chapter will examine why the expectations generated by the above theory have not been borne out by the passage of time. To this end, the theory of consumer demand with variable preferences will be briefly reviewed and one possible explanation put forth for the apparent failure to the theory to fulfill the expectations it generated. The problems posed

2. The references are S. Ichimura, "A Critical Note on the Definition of Related Goods," *Review of Economic Studies*, vol. 18, 1950–1951, pp. 179–183; G. Tintner, "Complementarity and Shifts in Demand," *Metroeconomica*, vol. 4, no. 1, 1952, pp. 1–4; R. L. Basmann, "A Note on an Invariant Property of Shifts in Demand," *Metroeconomica*, vol. 6, no. 2, 1954; R. L. Basmann, *Application of Several Econometric Techniques to a Theory of Demand with Variable Tastes*, Iowa State College, Ames, Iowa: Ph.D. thesis, 1955; R. L. Basmann, "A Theory of Demand with Variable Consumer Preferences," *Econometrica*, vol. 24, no. 1, 1956, pp. 47–58.

by the analysis will naturally lead to the discussion of a somewhat different viewpoint of the economic aspects of consumer behavior.

Review of Previous Theory

Let X_i = quantity of ith good consumed (per unit time)

$\quad P_i$ = price of ith good

$\quad u$ = utility function of individual consumer

$\quad I$ = income of consumer

$\quad a$ = shift parameter, which summarizes the effects of preference changes.

The general method of approaching the problem was to assume that the individual's utility function shifts as a result of advertising, promotional efforts, product improvement, or new-product introduction.[3] Mathematically, this implies introducing a shift parameter into the utility function.[4]

This implies, following Tintner, that an integrable utility function for an individual can be written[5] $u = u(X_1, X_2,..., X_n; a)$. The decision problem to be solved by the consumer is to maximize u, subject to the budget constraint, assuming the prices $P_1,..., P_n$ and income I are taken as given by the individual in question. The question is, How do the decisions of the consumer shift with

3. The use of this model to analyze the effects of new-product introduction requires further comment. Such a use implies an extension of the model to explain the meaning of new-product introduction in the context of the model. A brief summary of one possible extension may be given. Let the number of industries in the market be subjected to a birth-and-death process, under the constraint that the number of births (new products) equals the number of deaths (products withdrawn from the market that were previously in it). Examine one of these changes. (Cf. H. A. Simon, *Models of Men*, John Wiley & Sons, Inc., New York, 1957, chap. 9.)

4. To simplify the analysis it is assumed that all new products introduced replace old ones so that the total number of products in the market remains the same.

5. Tintner, *op. cit.*

shifts in a, i.e., with changes in the consumer preferences for goods?

Before proceeding into a detailed analysis of this question, it is necessary to justify interpreting the undoubtedly complex effects of such phenomena as advertising, product quality improvement, and so on, as "nothing more" than a shift parameter.

The parameter may be interpreted as a summary parameter representing the effect of the consumption of others upon the individual in question.[6] It is well known that economic decisions of individuals in situations of the type under discussion are dependent at least in part upon learning from other individuals. This phenomenon is usually called *personal influence* or *opinion leadership* and is quite well documented, especially with respect to the increase in use of innovations.[7] This model therefore views the process of preference change through the device of inter-personal interaction and family decision making with individual effects and exogenous variables effects buried behind the determination of the diffusion shift parameter. Thus the model represents a comparative-static analysis of the diffusion phenomenon from the viewpoint of individual consumer decision making.

This type of model may well seem awkward; however, how better to represent the effects of preference shifts in comparative-static analysis remains an unsolved problem. Thus, the use of a shift parameter can be simply and clearly justified.

The analysis that follows implicitly assumes two further things: first, that any shift in the production function occasioned by the employment of a preference-shifting device by the firm is neutral in its effects on demand, and second, that in the case

6. See W. F. Massy, *Innovation and Market Penetration*, Massachusetts Institute of Technology, Cambridge, Massachusetts: Ph.D. thesis, 1960, p. 44, and J. S. Duesenberry, *Income, Saving and the Theory of Consumer Behavior*, Harvard University Press, Cambridge, Massachusetts, 1949.

7. E. M. Rogers, *Diffusion of Innovations*, The Free Press, New York, 1962; H. F. Lionberger, *Adoption of New Ideas and Practices*, Iowa State University Press, Ames, Iowa, 1960.

of new-product introduction the effect of the old product being withdrawn from the market is negligible, so that the shift parameter actually does represent the effects of the new product. It is now possible to proceed with a description of the model under consideration.

As is well known, if the utility function is maximized under the condition that the budget equation holds, then

$$\sum_{i=1}^{n} P_i X_i = I \qquad (\textbf{1-1})$$

and

$$-\lambda P_j + u_j = 0 \qquad j = 1, \ldots, n. \qquad (\textbf{1-2})$$

Where there are n products, λ represents the marginal utility of money, and $u_j = \partial u / \partial X_j$, the marginal utility of X_j.

The necessary and sufficient conditions for a maxima imply that

$$U = \begin{bmatrix} u_{ij} & u_i \\ u_j & 0 \end{bmatrix} \qquad (\textbf{1-3})$$

is negative definite, where $u_{ij} = \partial^2 u / \partial X_i \partial X_j$.

Present interest is, of course, upon the effects of changes in a upon (1-1) and (1-2). Therefore, we next differentiate (1-1) and (1-2) with respect to a, obtaining

$$\sum_{i=1}^{n} P_i X_{ia} = 0 \qquad (\textbf{1-4})$$

and

$$-P_j \lambda_a + \sum_{i=1}^{n} u_{ji} X_{ia} = -u_{ja}, \qquad (\textbf{1-5})$$

where

$$\lambda_a = \partial \lambda / \partial a$$

$$X_{ia} = \partial X_i / \partial a$$

$$u_{ia} = \partial u_i / \partial a.$$

The expression u_{ia} represents the change in the marginal utility of commodity i caused by a small shift in the parameter a, which represents the shift in the utility function arising from an alteration of the consumer's preferences.

From (1-2), $P_j = u_j/\lambda$. Hence (1-4) and (1-5) may be re-written using (1-2) as

$$\sum_{i=1}^{n} X_i X_{ia} = 0 \qquad (1\text{-}6)$$

$$u_j \frac{-\lambda_a}{\lambda} + \sum_{i=1}^{n} u_{ji} X_{ia} = -u_{ja} \qquad j = 1, \ldots, n. \qquad (1\text{-}7)$$

This system can be solved in terms of the determinant $|U|$ and its cofactors. The variables to be solved for are, of course, X_{ia} and λ_a. Let U_{ji} denote the cofactor of U derived from the element u_{ji}. That is,

$$U^{-1} = \begin{bmatrix} u_{ij} & u_i \\ u_j & 0 \end{bmatrix}^{-1} = \frac{1}{|U|} \begin{bmatrix} U_{ij} & U_{n+1,i} \\ U_{i,n+1} & U_{n+1,n+1} \end{bmatrix}. \qquad (1\text{-}8)$$

The solution is

$$\lambda_a = \frac{\lambda \cdot \sum_{i=1}^{n} U_{n+1,i} u_{ia}}{|U|} \qquad (1\text{-}9)$$

$$X_{ja} = \frac{-\sum_{i=1}^{n} U_{ji} u_{ia}}{|U|} \qquad (1\text{-}10)$$

As is well known,

$$S_{ij} = \frac{\lambda U_{ij}}{|U|} \qquad (1\text{-}11)$$

where (1-11) is the Slutsky equation.

If it is assumed that when $i \neq j$, $u_{ia} = 0$, and (1-11) is sub-stituted into (1-10), the result is

$$X_{ja} = \frac{-S_{ij} u_{ja}}{\lambda}. \qquad (1\text{-}12)$$

Thus, if $u_{ja} > 0$, $X_{ja} > 0$. In other words, if it is assumed that the change in preferences has increased the marginal utility of the product, leaving unaffected the marginal utilities of the other products, then this change will increase demand for the product under question.

Basmann has shown that this result is qualitatively invariant under valid transformations of the utility function.[8] He has also explored the effects of such a shift taking into account the existence of substitutes and complements for the product.[9] However, this result leaves unanswered the question of how the preference shift alters the relative slopes of the price and income consumption lines, upon which the demand elasticities depend in the usual analysis.

This question has been studied by Massy. Massy shows that the derivatives of the substitution terms S_{ij} with respect to a are not necessarily invariant in sign to valid changes in the utility function. He also demonstrates there are strong indications that $\partial^2 X/\partial a\partial I$ and $\partial^2 X/\partial a\partial P$ are also not sign invariant.[10]

Massy's method of reaching these conclusions may be briefly described. His strategy is first to differentiate S_{ij} with respect to a, then to differentiate the conditions for consumer equilibrium with respect to P_1 and I, and then, again with respect to a, to solve the resulting system for the two relevant cross partials, given in (1-14), combine the two solutions to yield $\partial S_{ij}/\partial a$, and finally to prove the result is not invariant for valid transformations of the utility function.

He begins with the well-known result that

$$S_{ij} = \frac{\partial X_i}{\partial P_j} + \frac{\partial X_i}{\partial I} X_j. \qquad (1\text{-}13)$$

8. Basmann, "A Note on an Invariant Property of Shifts in Demand."

9. Basmann, "A Theory of Demand with Variable Consumer Preferences."

10. These results are quite well known but seem not to have been made available in the general literature. The exception is Massy, *op. cit.*

Then

$$\frac{\partial S_{ij}}{\partial a} = \frac{\partial^2 X_i}{\partial a \partial P_j} + X_j \frac{\partial^2 X_i}{\partial a \partial I} + \frac{\partial X_j}{\partial a} \frac{\partial X_i}{\partial I}. \qquad (1\text{-}14)$$

The problem is to find expressions for $\partial^2 X_i/\partial a \partial P_j$ and $\partial^2 X_i/\partial a \partial I$ in terms of known utility function and demand expressions. Following the process described above, Massy finds

$$\frac{\partial^2 X_1}{\partial a \partial I} = \frac{1}{\lambda^2}\left(\sum_h \sum_j \sum_k S_{1h} X_{j1} u_{hjk} \sum_R S_{Rk} u_{Ra} - \lambda \sum_h \sum_j S_{1h} X_{j1} u_{1ja}\right)$$

$$(1\text{-}15)$$

and

$$\frac{\partial^2 X_1}{\partial a \partial P_j} = \frac{1}{\lambda^2}\left[\sum_h \sum_j \sum_k S_{1h} X_{jP_1} u_{hjk} \sum_R S_{Rk} u_{Ra}\right.$$

$$-\lambda \sum_h \sum_j S_{1h} X_{jP_1} u_{1ja} + \lambda^2 S_{11} \sum_R \frac{D_{n+1,R} u_{Ra}}{|D|}$$

$$\left.-\lambda \frac{D_{n+1,1}}{|D|}\left(\sum_R S_{iR} u_{Ra}\right)\right], \qquad (1\text{-}16)$$

where $u_{hjk} = \partial u_{ij}/\partial X_k$
$\quad u_{1ja} = \partial u_{ij}/\partial a$
$\quad D = \begin{bmatrix} u_{ij} & P_i \\ P_j & 0 \end{bmatrix},$

all indices summed over the n products. An expression for $\partial S_{11}/\partial a$ in terms of known functions of utility functions and demand expressions may be written from (1-15) and (1-16) rather than from the formal notation of (1-14).

The final question is whether the expressions (1-15), (1-16), and therefore (1-14) are invariant in sign for valid transformations of the utility function.

Consider a valid transformation from the utility function ϕ, where $u = F(\phi)$, $F' > 0$

$$u_i = F'(\phi_i)$$
$$u_{ij} = F'\phi_{ij} + F''\phi_i\phi_j$$
$$u_{ijk} = F'\phi_{ijk} + F''(\phi_{ij}\phi_k + \phi_{ik}\phi_j + \phi_{jk}\phi_i) + F'''\phi_i\phi_j\phi_k$$
$$\lambda = F'\lambda_\phi.$$

Since the sign and magnitude of F'' and F''' are arbitrary for a valid transformation, the signs and magnitudes of nonzero expressions in which they appear are also arbitrary, thus disproving the sign invariance of any such equation. Thus, invariance is found by determining if quantities in ϕ involving F'' and F''' go to zero after the transformations in (1-15) and (1-16).

It is clear that this is not the case and that it follows that (1-15), (1-16), and $\partial S_{11}/\partial a$ cannot be proved to be sign invariant. Massy concludes that this result shows the theoretical impossibility of attempts to deduce even the signs of changes in substitution effects.

Probably the best summary of this result would be to say that the theory is not a good predictor of situations that can be characterized in the manner presented. It is important to note that this result indicates that changes *of the type under consideration* cannot be explained or predicted merely by the construction of a constantly shifting demand curve for the individual consumer. Knowledge of the demand curve of the previous time period and the shift parameter is not enough to define the demand curve for the individual for the current period.

Discussion

The preceding result is not too surprising if it is considered carefully. The original theory it derives from rests on the assumption of stable tastes. This assumption is then relaxed, being replaced by the added assumption that tastes change and the direction of their change is known. This is all the additional information assumed to be required. It would be somewhat amazing if a great deal could be said about consumer behavior in such situations.

Writing in 1934, J. A. Schumpeter stated, "'Static' analysis is not only unable to predict the consequences of discontinuous changes (such as new product introduction) in the traditional way of doing things; it can neither explain the occurrence of such productive revolutions nor the phenomena which accompany them."[11] It can be seen that this indictment is largely correct in the context of the model developed in the previous section. That this is so provides an additional and compelling reason to attempt an investigation of consumer behavior from a different point of view.[12]

Introduction to an Alternative Viewpoint

The natural question at this point is, What is a reasonable alternative point of view?[13] Put another way, Is it customary and reasonable to expect consumers to act so as to maximize their satisfaction subject to constraints imposed on their behavior by their income and the prices of the goods available?[14] One of the basic assumptions underlying the good sense of the simple maximizing behavior of the traditional model is that people and

11. J. A. Schumpeter, *The Theory of Economic Development*, Harvard University Press, Cambridge, Massachusetts, 1934, p. 62.
12. It must be noted that the situation is not the same when innovations in methods of producing goods are considered. In this case, Schumpeter seems to have been partly overstating the lack of power of accepted economic theory. (Cf. W. Fellner, "Does the Market Direct the Relative Factor-Saving Effects of Technological Progress?" in *The Rate and Direction of Inventive Activity: Economic and Social Factors*, Princeton University Press, Princeton, New Jersey, 1962, and E. Mansfield, "Comment," in *ibid.*)
13. This discussion draws on George H. Haines, Jr., "A Theory of Market Behavior After Innovation," *Management Science*, vol. 10, no. 4, July, 1964.
14. The evidence for the usefulness of this viewpoint is overwhelming. See, for example, H. Wald, with L. Jureen, *Demand Analysis*, John Wiley & Sons, Inc., New York, 1953.

firms either learn over time without outside encouragement or are forced by competitive or social pressure to learn.[15] It has been customary to accept this as one of the reasons that the traditional model is sensible; such a statement is usually the end of the matter.

It is also reasonable to assume that after the individual's preference pattern has been altered, a period of time lapses before a new preference pattern that will be stable in the future is formed. During this period of time, one could expect that people would continue to attempt to act rationally. But now a different meaning must be attached to the word *rational*. Some rule of thumb to guide behavior must be postulated that implies rationality. The rule of thumb that is proposed is the following: A sensible motivation for the development of a model of consumer behavior is that people can learn, i.e., in a loose sense are capable of adaptive behavior. Indeed, if this is not accepted, it is hard to understand how it is that the individual consumer ever achieves a satisfaction-maximizing consumption pattern. To make such an assumption is, of course, only the beginning. But before proceeding it may be instructive to note some other alternatives.

As has been seen, it is not enough just to assume simple maximizing behavior and a preference shift and to attempt to analyze the situation in terms of comparative statics. Such a procedure leaves significant questions unanswered.

Another possible method of attack is to assume, in the aggregate, a simple response on the part of consumers to

15. A. Alchian, "Uncertainty, Evolution, and Economic Theory," *Journal of Political Economy*, June, 1950, pp. 211–221.

Learning is a technical term to psychologists. It is useful to note two definitions of this term: "Learning is defined as the process by which an activity originates or is changed through responding to a situation." Alternatively, "Learning is defined as the persisting changes as a result of practice; the process by which new or altered behavior comes about as a result of prior responses, provided the changes cannot be attributed to growth or to temporary changes in the state of the organism (as in fatigue or under drugs)." *Source:* Ernest R. Hilgard, *Introduction to Psychology*, 2nd ed., Harcourt, Brace & World, Inc., New York, 1957, pp. 23 and 583, respectively.

educational efforts on the part of the firm. One then takes data and fits them to such a reasonable probability distribution. This has been done.[16] The question then is to assign some sort of meaning to the results and to show that they make any sense. This has not been done, although later in Chapter 5 we will discuss the relation between Ehrenberg's work and the central theory of this book, arguing that the theory to be developed can be used to give meaning to Ehrenberg's empirical studies.

Another approach recently proposed is to redefine the concept of the utility function and attempt then to reconstruct the theory.[17] This is, in fact, part of what is proposed in this book. Yet this approach retains the basic comparative-static assumption that time is not important, whereas it may very well be that time is of the essence. This is undoubtedly an empirical question that the passage of time and work may solve. Without demeaning such an approach nor necessarily implying it is unreasonable, it may be conjectured that something stronger and no more or less radical may serve better.

So it seems reasonable to reject these alternatives, and proceed on the belief that a sensible assumption for the development of a theory of consumer behavior during a period of shifting consumer preference patterns is to assume that consumers are capable of learning.[18]

To derive a reasonable model it is necessary to begin by considering an idealized consumer in action, shopping for nondurable goods. Assume the consumer shops once a week, always on the same day, and before shopping reads advertisements about

16. For example, B. Benjamin, W. P. Jolly, and J. Maitland, "Operational Research and Advertising: Theories of Response," *Operational Research Quarterly*, vol. 11, no. 4, December, 1960. One of the best-known studies of this type is A. S. C. Ehrenberg, "The Pattern of Consumer Purchases," *Applied Statitics*, vol. 8, 1959, pp. 26–41.

17. Kelvin J. Lancaster, "A New Approach to Consumer Theory," *Journal of Political Economy*, vol. LXXIV, no. 2, April, 1966.

18. Rogers (*op. cit.*, p. 77) states, "The process by which innovations are adopted by individuals is essentially a limited example of how any type of learning takes place."

nondurable products in an effort to gain information about the market. Further, assume the consumer always shops in the same store and that, when shopping, walks all the aisles in the supermarket and tries to look at the products displayed. Suppose there is a new product on one of the shelves, say, the first heavy-duty liquid detergent ever produced. The consumer may be motivated to purchase it merely by seeing something new on the shelves, picking it up, and reading the label. Or perhaps the consumer has seen an advertisement for it, or had a neighbor or her husband suggest she try it, and was looking for the product. At any rate, assume that the product is purchased.

The consumer then carries it home and tries it. From this trial use, the consumer gains experience with the product or not. If the product gives satisfaction in use, the consumer may try it again. And so on, until at last the consumer is completely used to the formerly new product and no longer regards it as new or different when seeing it on the shelf. It becomes just another good, like all the rest.

The above description brings out some simple, but extremely important, points. The first is that the consumer controls by his or her actions whether the product is tried. Second, that the reward in purchasing the product to the consumer is inherent in what occurs when the product is used. Third, the product, whether it is eventually used or not, over time acquires in the consumer's mind the characteristic of having always been there, i.e., the product is not looked at by the consumer as being new in the sense that he or she is unsure about what satisfiaction the product will bring in use. Note that it is by no means necessary that the product be new in a technical sense, that is, just placed on the market. All that is required is that it be new to the purchaser, and such newness may arise from product promotions, advertising, or other marketing actions of the firm, as well as from a technically new product.

To summarize, the crucial aspects of the situation are that it is postulated that consumers behave toward a new product in such a way that (1) the events of purchasing, using, and gaining information about the product are controlled by the consumer, and (2), given (1), that consumers learn about the product from their experience with it and, perhaps, from uses suggested by other persons or in advertising for the product that the consumer has read.

The basic postulate that the preceding discussion had led to may now be stated. It is postulated that the process of increase or decrease in use of a product for which a favorable or unfavorable preference shift occurs may be modeled by assuming learning behavior on the part of the consumer, with the events taking place being controlled by the individual concerned.

Concrete Specification and the Possibilities of Empirical Refutation of the Postulate

The next issue to be dealt with is a discussion of the possibilities of specifying this stated postulate so that it may be empirically refuted.[19] This discussion will lead to a discussion of certain further implications of the postulate.[20]

As is well known, learning is an internal phenomenon. The decision process involved in the phenomenon may be directly studied by methods recently introduced. The methods involve the detailed study of learning at the individual level, the taking of protocols, and the construction of a specific theory in the form of a computer program.[21] This is an important point, for it

---

19. Haines, *op. cit.*, pp. 634–658.

20. This section presumes an elementary knowledge of psychological learning theory. See E. R. Hilgard, *Theories of Learning*, Appleton-Century-Crofts, New York, 1956, for such an introduction.

21. J. Feldman, "Computer Simulation of Cognitive Processes," chap. 15 of H. Borko, ed., *Computer Applications in the Behavioral Sciences*, Prentice-Hall, Inc., Englewood Cliffs, New Jersey, 1962, and E. A. Feigenbaum and J. Feldman, eds., *Computers and Thought*, McGraw-Hill Book Company, New York, 1963, contain a detailed discussion of the process, problems involved, and examples.

implies that the basic postulate may be directly tested.[22] Appendix A of this book, "A Study of the Problem of Building a Model to Simulate the Cognitive Processes of a Shopper in a Supermarket," by Robert H. King, represents discussion in detail of attempt to do just this: to test the basic postulate that shopping behavior involves learning. However, such a statement must not be taken to imply that such a task is easy, for as King's work demonstrates, this does not appear to be the case. In particular, as has been discussed by Clarkson, the task of actually verifying that such a simulation adequately describes reality is not a solved problem.[23] A further difficulty is that the basic theory of consumer behavior would then be constructed of two parts, each part consisting of a different analytical tool. It therefore seems sensible to attempt to construct a mathematical theory to conceptualize consumer behavior during the period of shifting preferences.

The important aspect of the situation lies in the consumer control of the purchase decision. It is therefore proposed to analyze the simplest case in which this key assumption can be maintained. This simplest case consists in abstracting from a possibly more realistic and surely more complex case in two directions: first, by assuming complete reinforcement instead of partial reinforcement, and second, by assuming that all consumers have simply a probability of purchase with the same parameters controlling their actions. Satisfaction derived from use of the product is then reflected in the values of the parameters that affect the consumers' actions.

Clearly this represents a considerable abstraction. However, this simplest case is an important one because it captures what is believed to be the essence of the situation under consideration. This is, to reiterate, that sales to consumers over the time period during which tastes shift are controlled by the consumers, and

22. See G. P. E. Clarkson, "Verification and the Function of Laws in Micro-Economics," *Industrial Management Review*, vol. 4, no. 1, 1962, pp. 41–58.
23. G. P. E. Clarkson, *Portfolio Selection: A Simulation of Trust Investment*, Prentice-Hall, Inc., Englewood Cliffs, New Jersey, 1962.

that a reasonable assumption about consumer behavior in such a case is that consumers learn.

Once these assumptions have been stated, a great deal has been said. For a mathematical theory does exist that purports to describe such behavior. It was proposed by Bush and Mosteller and adapted in generalized form by Kuehn to the brand shifting of consumers among established brands of a product.[24] The essential details of this theory may be briefly reviewed as an overview of Chapters 2 and 3.

The basic elements of the model are as follows: There is a set of alternatives A_j and a set of outcomes O_k. An alternative-outcome pair (A_j, O_k) is called the event E_{jk}. The outcome determines the event in the case under consideration because it has been assumed that the consumer controls by his actions the resulting outcome. For example, suppose there is a consumer in a T maze. If he turns right, reward is always found; if he turns left, reward is never presented. The two responses are turning right, A_1, and turning left, A_2. Event E_1 is identified with turning right and finding reward, event E_2 with turning left and finding no reward. The event includes the response and the outcome, but the outcome of the trial is always determined by the response made by the consumer. Event E_1 occurs when A_1 occurs, E_2 when A_2 occurs. This case Bush and Mosteller call the case of subject-controlled events. The similarity between the above example and the previously discussed hypothetical, idealized consumer is clear.

The state of the organism that is about to make the choice on a given trial is described by a probability vector, each component of which gives the probability of choosing a particular alternative on the next trial. When an event occurs on a particular

24. References are R. R. Bush and F. Mosteller, *Stochastic Models for Learning*, John Wiley & Sons, Inc., New York, 1955; A. A. Kuehn, *An Analysis of the Dynamics of Consumer Behavior and Its Implications for Marketing Management*, Carnegie Institute of Technology, Pittsburgh, Pennsylvania: Ph.D. thesis, 1958; A. A. Kuehn, "A Model for Budgeting Advertising," in F. M. Bass et al., eds., *Mathematical Models and Methods in Marketing*, Richard D. Irwin, Inc., Homewood, Illinois, 1961.

trial, this alters the probability vector. Specifically, for each event denoted E_{jk} that occurs on trial a,

$$p(n + 1) = T_{jk}p(n).$$

The operators T_{jk} are linear stochastic matrices. When the foregoing equivalence between responses and events is assumed, the probability of a given event on a particular trial is not constant over trials. Further, the conditional probabilities are not constant. For example, the conditional probability of event E_1 on trial $n + 1$, given that E_1 occurred on trial n, is not constant; it is equal to $Q_1p(n)$, where Q_1 refers to the first element of T_{jk}. This probability $Q_1p(n)$, depends on the previous decisions and the number of trials. This result implies that a Markov chain with states representing brands purchased is not an appropriate model of consumer learning behavior.

Next, it is sensible to enquire into the qualitative characteristics of the model that has been presented. To do this it is useful to note that the vector T_ip may be written

$$T_ip = \alpha_ip + (1 - \alpha_i)\lambda_i$$

where the sum of the elements of the p vectors equals one. Additionally, $0 \le \alpha_i \le 1$. If $\alpha_i < 0$ but more than -1, oscillatory behavior results. This would not be an expected situation in the context of consumer behavior.

It can be immediately seen that the λ_i constitutes stable equilibrium probabilities of the purchase and the α_i constitutes a measure of how rapid (over trials) the approach to equilibrium is from the initial probability. This is a very simple result. Before discussing its implications, it is of some use to ask what is known about how these parameters are set. The present author has investigated the hypothesis that, in the case of new-product introduction, the parameter values can be regarded as linear functions of marketing variables controlled by the firm (e.g., price, advertising, promotion, and so on).[25] The results do not appear to suggest that this is a useful hypothesis. Kuehn has suggested a somewhat more complicated relationship that basically regards the λ_1 as a cardinal measure of product value share.[26] The function he proposes is

$$\lambda_i = b_1(PD)_i + b_2 \frac{(PDA)_i}{\sum(PDA)_i},$$

where $\sum(PD) = 1$ by normalization

$$P_i = \frac{KP_i'P_i^{-E}}{\sum\limits_i P_i^{-E}}$$

b_1, b_2, K, E = constants

P_i' = relative appeal to consumers of product i

P_i = price of product i

D_i = Measure of effectiveness of distribution and display space in retail stores of product i

A_i = advertising, weighted for effectiveness, of brand i.

All of these variables are measurable in principle. It is most important to note that P_i', the relative appeal to consumers of product i, is taken to be a measurable quantity in this theory. It is not an ordinal utility function. This carries with it the equally strong statement that the theory to be developed in detail in this book will enable measurements to be made to determine whether consumer preferences have shifted. Thus the theory carries within it the ability to allow ascertainment of when the ordinary, simple economic theory of consumer behavior is likely to be not useful. Finally, it can be seen that this means that the theory developed here has more built into it than the usual theory of consumer behavior, and thus it may yield stronger results. The issue of measuring P_i' and the results therefrom are discussed in appropriate detail later in this book. It should be noted at this point,

25. Haines, *op. cit.* These results are reviewed in appropriate detail in Chapter 3 of this book.
26. Kuehn, "A Model for Budgeting Advertising."

however, that this model has stimulated work on how actually to achieve measurement of these variables: Kuehn and Day have discussed how to obtain a measure of the relative appeal of products to consumers, Kuehn and Weiss have studied how D_i could be measured in principle, and Silk and Miller have shown how to achieve a measurement of advertising volume weighted for effectiveness.[27] The Kuehn formulation has the further advantage of being able to show how shifts in variables qualitatively affect the equilibrium value—that is, it allows comparative-statics analysis to be performed. To discuss in further detail what causes specific parameter values to obtain in specific instances is beyond the scope of this chapter, but it should be pointed out that the existing research clearly indicates that the parameter values do not just magically appear but are the result of market forces and consumer tastes.

It is now time to return to an examination of the qualitative characteristics of the proposed model. At equilibrium, the consumer has a constant probability of purchasing each product. This probability, however, given the Kuehn interpretation of the meaning of λ_i, may be taken to represent the value share of the ith product purchased by the consumer. But, as is well known, the usual theory of consumer behavior also generates value shares of the ith product that are constant, other things being constant.[28] Thus the qualitative characteristics are such as to suggest that at final equilibrium, as at initial equilibrium, the traditional theory of consumer behavior holds and may constitute a sufficient explanation of consumer behavior. The qualifier "may" is necessary, it should be noted, because the Kuehn formulation

27. References are A. A. Kuehn and R. L. Day, "Strategy of Product Quality," *Harvard Business Review*, vol. 40, November–December, 1962, pp. 100–110, A. A. Kuehn and D. L. Weiss, "Marketing Analysis Training Exercise," *Behavioral Science*, vol. 10, no. 1, January, 1965, pp. 51–67, and A. J. Silk and S. Miller, "Changes in Market Share and Advertising Strategy: A Re-examination," Graduate School of Business Administration, UCLA, Los Angeles, California: mimeographed manuscript, August, 1965.

28. H. Theil, "The Information Approach to Demand Analysis," *Econometrica*, vol. 33, no. 1, 1965, pp. 67–87.

does not preclude the price of a good from entering the consumers' ordinal utility function.

The Relation of the Model and the Traditional Economic Model

The relation between the model presented here and the traditional economic model is at once quite simple and quite complex. Obviously, the model discussed here presumes a utility tree. In such cases, the first decision a consumer makes is how income should be allocated among budget branches. Each budget allotment is then spent optimally on the commodities of its branch, with no further reference to purchases in other branches.[29] The set of brands summed over in the Kuehn formulation is simply the set of brands at the end of the branch.

Note that branching is assumed to be much finer in the Kuehn analysis than has been customary to assume in theoretical economic analysis. Given this fact, at equilibrium both the traditional economic analysis and the model of this book generate the same information: a value share. This correspondence may be seen by explicitly writing out the relation, where PS_i denotes average purchasing size of the ith brand,

$$w_i = \frac{P_i q_i}{\mu} = \left(b_{PD}(PD^{\varepsilon_D})_i + \frac{(PD^{\varepsilon_D} A^{\varepsilon_A})}{\sum_i (PD^{\varepsilon_D} A^{\varepsilon_A})_i} \right) PS_i.$$

Thus it is quite obvious that there is no conflict between the two theories. To reiterate the point: The two theories simply are designed to answer different types of questions. Further, the influence of consumer income μ can now be seen to be merely the usual influence of income, i.e., it will affect the average purchase size.

29. Robert H. Strotz, "The Empirical Implications of a Utility Tree," *Econometrica*, vol. 26, no. 3, pp. 269–280.

Conclusion

This chapter has argued that there is a specific class of problems, arising from marketing efforts on the part of the firm and from family decision making, that the traditional economic theory of consumer behavior does not adequately explain. The class of such problems has been explicitly defined, and an alternative theory has been proposed and briefly discussed to explain consumer behavior in such situations. Finally, it has been argued that the alternative theory leads inevitably to the reestablishment of a situation in which the traditional economic theory of consumer behavior is once again adequate to explain consumer behavior. We are now ready to proceed with the detailed discussion of the alternative theory.

A Study of the Problem of Building a Model to Simulate the Cognitive Processes of a Shopper in a Supermarket

Robert H. King

The Problem

This section will be opened with a quotation from Hunt[1] because it seems appropriate to the circumstances surrounding the reason for writing this report.

As we conceive it, the scientific study of a problem consists of (*a*) a description of a particular phenomenon in a precise, unambiguous, and perhaps abstract manner, and (*b*) certain statements about the relations between different aspects of the phenomenon of interest. The description must be precise enough to be given empirical reference so that the truth or falsity of the relational statements can be determined. Such a conception of science assumes the existence of a language on which we can place certain requirements. The language must be unambiguous, so that it is clear what a particular statement implies concerning the relation between

1. Earl B. Hunt, *Concept Learning*, John Wiley & Sons, Inc., New York, 1962.

different entities. No natural language adequately satisfies this criterion, although it might be possible to construct a spoken language that would (Brown, 1960). At the same time, a language must be suitable for describing the problem at hand. The scientist usually, if not always, begins work on a problem with a vague desire to "understand something" about a real world problem. If he cannot describe his interests, the precision of his language is irrelevant.

In this study, the author finds an identity between himself and the statement cited above. That is, the author is beginning work on a problem with a vague desire to "understand something" about a real-world problem. This desire may be described as vague because the problem, in total, is of very large proportions. Simply stated, the total problem is that of creating a computer program that can be used to simulate the thought processes involved in the consumer's efforts to fill his shopping cart with items from a supermarket. Ultimately, the test of success for this program would call for placing the computer and a human being within the same "shopping environment" and comparing the results of the computer's decisions against those of the human being's. But how does one arrive at such a program?

As pointed out in Feigenbaum and Feldman,[2] the researcher who wishes to simulate cognitive processes begins with an interest in a certain area of human activity. He then focuses his attention on the human behavior involved in carrying out a specific task related to that area of interest, for his primary goal is to construct a preliminary model of the behavior associated with that task. He may obtain an idea of the activities involved in the task either by observing the actions of the human being involved in the given process or by asking him to explain, in detail, what he is doing while performing the task. But the ultimate goal of the researcher is to find an ordered sequence of the basic processes used in the task which, when provided with suitable information,

2. E. A. Feigenbaum and J. Feldman, eds., *Computers and Thought*, McGraw-Hill Book Company, New York, 1963, p. 275.

will produce behavior indistinguishable from the behavior produced by human beings when they are provided with comparable information. Thus an information-processing model of the human shopper's behavior in filling his market basket would consist of a sequence of the basic processes performed by the shopper while fulfilling this task.

The ultimate goal of research in this topic is thus seen to be the creation of a generalized computer program that can be used to predict a given shopper's decisions in filling his shopping cart in a supermarket. To do this, the simulation model must provide for:

1. Inputting the large variety of data that serve to define the shopper's history, or background.
2. Inputting the detailed data that define the shopping environment within which the task is to be performed.
3. Inputting sufficient data to define the shopper's goals for the present shopping trip.

The test of the model would consist of running the program against this given data and comparing the model's decisions against those of the shopper who performed his task in a real-life environment. But as previously noted, the difficulties involved in creating such a program will put this level of accomplishment some distance into the future.

The purpose of this study, therefore, is to lay the groundwork for future studies by attempting to identify and define the task being performed by an actual shopper in a real-life shopping environment. The basis for this study is a number of tape recorded protocols that were obtained from actual shopping experiences. More detailed comments concerning these protocols will be made later. The tasks being performed by the subject in these shopping experiences have been identified and defined by the author through the use of a flow diagram. This flow diagram is hypothesized to reflect all the actions demonstrated by the subject in her detailed protocol. The reader should view this flow diagram as an abstraction of the shopping process in general, rather than as a step-by-step description of the given subjects' actions during a single shopping tour. The attempt has been to hypothesize a general set of procedures and processes that any shopper will employ if his or her goals are to be attained. This flow diagram will be compared, in a number of instances, to the protocol from which it was derived in order to show the relationship between the hypothesized process and specific actions taken by the subject. Finally, the paper will conclude by suggesting areas of future study that need to be undertaken before the ultimate goal of creating an actual computer program may be reached.

The Protocols

This study was begun by taping a number of protocols with several subjects in actual shopping environments. The first and last of these five protocols were made with the same subject, whereas the others were conducted with three different individuals.

The original instructions to the subjects were as follows: "The purpose of this protocol is to examine a typical shopper's methods, reasons, and habits, for selecting a variety of items from the myriad of those on the grocery-store shelves. As we proceed with the shopping tour, I will, from time to time, ask you·what you are now doing and why you are selecting the item that you have selected. I would like you to try to explain, first, why you have selected the type of food, second, why you are choosing the brand you are choosing, and third, what is the method by which you normally approach a shopping tour. That is, do you start at the meat counter and work in a certain direction, or do you start at vegetables and go some other direction? In other words, whatever your normal habits are. Any comments concerning these factors would be appreciated. So, with this, we will now begin the shopping." These instructions did not lead to obtaining data that had any face validity.

The second technique employed in taking a protocol and used in the protocol reported here was simply to give the subject the microphone and ask her to verbalize, fully and completely, any and all thoughts that ran through her mind as we proceeded through the store. In order to ensure that the subject would not covertly decide that a given fleeting thought was of no consequence, she was repeatedly encouraged to state explicitly her every thought, insofar as humanly possible, no matter how trivial or irrelevant that thought might appear to her at the time. The reader will be able to observe for himself just how successful we were in obtaining as complete a protocol as seems humanly possible. Not only did we capture a large number of relevant thoughts that might have otherwise been lost, but we also captured a glimpse of the subjects' total personality. This was rather unexpected by the author, and he has attempted to convey, as closely as is possible in writing, this personality by spelling the subject's words as actually used in conversation. Furthermore, several comments and symbols have been injected to convey the context and atmosphere within which many of the remarks were made. It is hoped that full disclosure in this matter will make it possible for others to analyze the protocol and, perhaps, gain insight into the problem that the author may have missed.

Since the fifth and final protocol was found to contain the most accurate and complete information, this protocol was used as the exclusive basis upon which the shopping-process flow diagram, Figure A-1, was constructed. This protocol was therefore typed in final form and made a part of the body of this report.

Before leaving this subject of protocols, the author would like to make an observation. Mr. Benjamin Kleinmuntz,[3] who wrote an article on clinical information processing in the December, 1965, issue of *Datamation Magazine*, has reported similar ideas concerning the importance of taking protocols in a proper fashion. He states on page 43, for example, that, "Perhaps the

---

3. Benjamin Kleinmuntz, "Clinical Information Processing," *Datamation*, December, 1965.

most important lesson learned from this project was that the clinician can be forced to make public and explicit his problem-solving strategies." A little later on he backs this up by saying, "The major problem in this particular approach [taking protocols] to studying the person at work, is that very often the expert in a particular specialty such as MMPI, EEG, and EKG interpretation actually thinks that he is using some special subliminal cues in arriving at his profile decisions. I had to convince my specialist that if the cues were subliminal, then he probably could not perceive them; and if he could not perceive them, maybe they were not worth worrying about. If the expert buys that explanation, you still have the additional problem of getting him to report continually about the supraliminal cues to which he is reacting. This takes persistant coaxing and nudging—which was not so bad because it served to keep both the expert and me awake."

Feigenbaum and Feldman[4] have also pointed out that there are difficult problems involved in discerning the mental processes underlying the overt behavior of a human being in a given task.

It seems, therefore, that any advantages resulting from the techniques used in taking the present protocol could have significant implications for the field of artificial intelligence. In the interest of scientific accuracy, the author feels obligated to state that his relationship with the subject and the inherent personality of the subject could have had a significant influence on the quality of the protocol thus obtained. In this instance, the subject and her family are very close friends of the author and his family. This factor served to establish an immediate rapport between these parties. It is also noted that the subject's inherently warm and friendly personality has undoubtedly played a large part in contributing to the success of this effort. Finally, it is noted that the problem to which the subject was addressing herself was connected with a natural part of everyday living, wherein the

4. Feigenbaum and Feldman, *loc. cit.*

rules governing her actions were largely a matter of her own choosing. This is opposed to those situations in which the subject is required to perform a mental process while bounded by an externally imposed set of rigorous rules over which he has no control. An example of this latter situation may be seen in Clarkson's[5] model of the trust investment process, where the subject is bounded by a finite and rigorous set of decision rules to be used in making his investment decision. For this reason, it is suggested that the free-flowing tempo of the following protocol may be more difficult to reproduce in protocols taken for cases where the problem areas are more rigidly bounded. On the other hand, it is this aspect of the situation that most clearly points out the potential contributions of this study. In general, previous work in the simulation of human thought processes has dealt with problems that impose external rules to an extent not found in the problem under consideration here.

Shopping Tour Protocol #5

INTERVIEWER:

(1)   This is Sunday evening, December 19, 1965, in the Thriftimart Shopping Center, and we are conducting an experimental shopping tour. From this point on, the subject will give most of the explanations for her actions during the tour.

SUBJECT:

(2)   Let's go to the meat department first. (Meat case was scanned.) They don't have any steaks or the roast like I want, so I have to ring the bell and get them to cut the meat special for me. (Meat man was off duty.) The sign

---

5. G. P. E. Clarkson, "A Model of the Trust Investment Process," in Feigenbaum and Feldman, *op. cit.* See also G. P. E. Clarkson, *The Theory of Consumer Demand*, Prentice-Hall, Inc., Englewood Cliffs, New Jersey, 1963.

says "Back at 8:00 P.M.," so let's start over here at the dairy counter.

(3)   Let's see—I'd better get some milk, because we'll be out of that in a few days. And I need some cottage cheese. I have to have Knudsen's small-curd cottage cheese. I'll look for some margarine, preferably Kraft, for baking. (All the above dairy items were obtained.)

(4)   Hey! Let's pick up some mix for some uh—hey—I got a check from my aunt for some Christmas cheer, so we've got to get some uh—what do we buy? No, not Like—what's that—no, not Bubble-Up—what's that other one? No, not 7-Up.

INTERVIEWER:

(5)   Uh—Squirt?

SUBJECT:

(6)   Something like that. I can't think of the stupid name of it. It comes in cartons like this, Bob, but I guess they just don't even have it. So, let's get 7-Up then, 'cause Jerry [her husband] likes that best. (Obtained.)

(7)   You know what? We're going to get some brandy, for Christmas, so we've gotta go get some of that Manhattan juice. (Obtained.)

(8)   We need the sweet vermouth for the Manhattans, don't we? (Interviewer replied, "Yes," and subject selected a brand.)

(9)   Let's get some uh—champagne to have—uh—you know, later on Christmas Eve, huh? Do you like pink or white best? Or the red? Or what?

INTERVIEWER:

(10)   Either one is O.K. with me.

SUBJECT:

(11)   I like the pink best.

INTERVIEWER:

(12)   O.K.

SUBJECT:

(13)   And I think we've had this brand, so we'll try it, huh?

(14)   And in case we make some uh—you know, Tom and Jerry's—we should have some egg nog, shouldn't we? (A brand was selected and the subject started looking for another liquor item.)

(15)   Yeah, they've got that Jack Bonet, but they've only got it in those little bitty old bottles! That's the best brand. (The subject didn't take the item because of her dissatisfaction with the packaging quantity.)

(16)   Let's go down this aisle and see if we can find some medical junk for my hands. (On the way, the subject spotted some toothpaste and remembered she needed some.)

(17)   Crest and Colgate are the same price so let's get Colgate—I've got a coupon for that.

(18)   You know, that poodle man that clips Inky [her dog], he said this stuff is good for any kind of sores. I wonder if it will help my uh—eczema. I'll give it a try, huh? Did I say the name of that stuff? It's Desitin—that's what I'm buying. (The subject then turned down an aisle on her way to find another item. She had not yet said what this item would be.)

(19)   Made a wrong turn—we don't need any light bulbs! (Laughter.) Right or left, I'll give you your choice. (Laughter.)

(20)   Let's go this way, I think I need a little cleanser. Help me look for that Comet, that's in those pretty bottles, you know, for in the bathroom. The little kind. Ah! There it is. Let's get that aqua one.

(21)   Hey! I need some S.O.S. Pads, too—just thought of it.

(22)   And I'd better get some wax paper, because I've got to pack all that candy in wax paper. Let's see which is the cheapest around here. Uh—I think this Zee will do.

That's pretty good. Think I'll keep going, I need some Kleenex. Hey! Do they mean this Springfield is on sale for 19¢? Oops! Well, I guess I dropped a few. (Laughter.) Hey! Let's get about three of them. Say, how do you like those man-size tissues? (Giggle.) They should have a sample out so we could see it.

(23)   Oh, and let's get some of these napkins for the holidays, huh? Hey! They've got two kinds—oh well, that's those holidays type. (While in this area, the subject saw some candles made in the form of Santa Claus.)

(24)   You know, I wonder if those stupid candles will fit in my candle holders. Shall we try it? Do you think those are cute?

INTERVIEWER:

(25)   Oh yeah—Santa Claus. (Chuckle.)

SUBJECT:

(26)   Where do we go from here? I've got to get Inky some Prime [dog food]. You know, he has been eating so much lately, we can't keep him in food. You know, the dog-food man only comes every other week. And I need some Frisky's Biscuits, too. (The dog-food items were obtained.)

(27)   How about helping me pick out some catnip for the cat, and then I've got to find a present for Inky for Christmas, too. Hey, what do you think of bringing the cat in and giving her catnip under the tree? (Laughter. With this, both parties began scanning the various cat products to find one with catnip as an ingredient.) We've just got to read the labels if we are going to find it. What's that thing? It's a little stocking for a kitty cat, but it doesn't say if it's got catnip in it. I mean, I don't know. I think they look kind of—Gee, we've got to have something to make it interesting Christmas Eve.

(28)   And you know those rawhide bones, do you see any of those? They are good for dogs, you know they can

eat 'em, they can—they can chew on them and it doesn't hurt them. And Inky likes those. I'll probably have to go to another store to find the cat a present.

INTERVIEWER:

(29)   (At this point, the interviewer asked for a description of rawhide bones so he could help find them.)

SUBJECT:

(30)   Oh, they are kind of like, they are tied in a knot—they are larger than that. (A similar item being held in the interviewers' hand.) Guess they just don't have them. I'll probably have to go to a pet store.

(31)   Look at the tip in that collar. I don't think it would pay to buy that one, would it? I can't find Inky a new collar for Christmas. Takes size 14, and boy, I'll tell ya— can't find a jeweled one, I thought maybe one of these would do for a while. (The latter-mentioned pet items were not obtained.)

(32)   (At this point, the subject contemplated a record purchase, but decided against it since there was a larger selection at the front of the store.)

SUBJECT:

(33)   I think they have got some at the front of the store, those records—you know—for 88¢. I'll pick up a couple of those for Claire [her daughter].

(34)   We're in the pickle aisle, and I don't know what—I gotta go up to the Food Giant to get the pickles, 'cause they got the best ones.

(35)   Say, can you play the stereo records on the monaural —you know, on the regular phonograph? Does it hurt them at all?

INTERVIEWER:

(36)   Yeah—uh, I mean no. You can do vice versa.

SUBJECT:

(37)   Guess we won't get any. We got to go back down this aisle 'cause Connie [interviewer's wife] wants some of that

Kikko Man, you know, Sauce, 'cause she wants to make that recipe I did, so I thought I'd look for it for her tonight. I don't know where the stuff is in this store, it should be with the soy sauce.

(38)   Let's go over another aisle. Maybe if we walk in, you know, the middle and look both ways, we might see it. (We didn't find it in the other aisle.)

(39)   Let's go down this aisle, 'cause I need sugar and flour. I almost used five pounds of sugar making that candy today. (Chuckle.) Can you get that Gold Medal flour, five pounds?

INTERVIEWER:

(40)   What was the other thing you just picked up?

SUBJECT:

(41)   Oh! I got sugar—C & H—I like that best.

(42)   Say, that man that's at the meat counter is the one I returned the pork roast to—you know, the pork roast that wasn't any good? (Giggle.)

INTERVIEWER:

(43)   Oh yeah?

SUBJECT:

(44)   Guess I don't want him to cut any special meat. (Laughter.) He'll probably remember me!

(45)   Looks like this place has had it today. Where are the ice-cream bars? Oh golly, let's uh—I guess I'll have to get this kind. Claire doesn't like them as well, but I guess it will be O.K. Oh, hey! Maybe I'd better not get that now, it will all melt before we get back home! (We then departed to get some ingredients for some cooking she was going to do.)

(46)   I don't think I need any of those chocolate chips, and—oh! but I do need some more almonds if I make some more toffee! (These ingredients reminded her of some toffee she wanted to make.)

(47)   They had better restock this place. I got the last

three bags of almonds. You know, you got to get those unblanched ones—you know. (At this point, the subject began to ponder where to go next.)

(48)   Guess I'd better consult the list. I know they got coffee on sale someplace.

INTERVIEWER:

(49)   You are consulting the shopping list, you say?

SUBJECT:

(50)   Yeah. Let's get some of this—they've got Chase & Sanborn. I'll get a couple pounds.

(51)   I think that professor should give me "A" for doing all this! (Laughter.)

(52)   Hold it a second, I need some instant coffee! I'm all out at work.

(53)   You know, you might still have a tape recorder, but I don't think you'll have a speaker [microphone] when we get out of here if I keep pulling on it like this. (Laughter.)

(54)   I'll get some Nescafe. We'll give that a try for a change.

(Note: Some time back, the interviewer asked the subject if he could hold the shopping list, as the subject had a tendency to crumple the list next to the microphone while holding both in the same hand. It was feared that excessive noise might be generated and degrade the recording quality.)

SUBJECT:

(55)   Now you got my list, and now I don't know what I want! (Laughter.)

(56)   Jerry needs some pipe cleaners. Help me find them.

INTERVIEWER:

(57)   How about these?

SUBJECT:

(58)   Yeah, that will be—what choice do we have? That's the only kind they got! (Laughter.) Two [packs] will do it.

1501950

(59)   Might as well get a carton of cigarettes—some of the Kents up there. I'll be out of those soon.

(60)   Let's see if we can find anything good down this aisle. I'll see if we can find some cheddar cheese. I've always eaten that. (On the way to the cheese counter, the subject made the following extemporaneous statement.)

(61)   Hey! If we taped everybody in the store, we would have a real variety. (Laughter.) I'd just kind of flip it up there [the microphone], you know—when they start talking. (Laughter.)

(62)   I'll take this mild American cheddar. (A comment was made by the subject at this point that is not understandable in the recording.)

(63)   Hey, maybe I'll get some of those beef pies, probably, for Thursday night. Jerry can fix those easily. I don't even know what we're going to have to eat this week. (The subject then left the freezer.)

INTERVIEWER:

(64)   Would you state the decision you just made, please?

SUBJECT:

(65)   Yes, Bobby, I get three Swanson pies. Inky and Groucho [the cat] can have something else. (Laughter.)

(66)   Hey! Look at this. This is that Leftsa. But I won't buy any, because I got a Leftsa recipe and I'm going to try and make it one of these days this week.

INTERVIEWER:

(67)   What in the world is Leftsa?

SUBJECT:

(68)   Oh, it's a Norwegian "dealy" [packaged item], you know, and you put butter and sugar on it, and roll it up, and the Norwegians eat it with fish. But I eat it just in place of bread for snacks and things.

INTERVIEWER:

(69)   Oh, it's almost like a tortilla or something.

SUBJECT:

(70)   Oh, no, no! This is made out of potatoes, mainly potatoes, and flour, and a little shortening, and milk—yeah, it looks like a tortilla, but it doesn't taste at all like it! (With this, both parties left the counter.)

(71)   What time is it? Do you think the meat man is back yet? Oh, only twenty till eight? Oh well—(the subject then turned her mind to something else.)

(72)   What kind of sandwiches do you like? I've gotta get something for sandwiches. Oh yeah, Claire likes that Thuringer junk, but I have a hard time finding it. I'll take all-meat summer sausage instead—because I can't find that Thuringer, they changed—Oscar Mayer's changed the way they package their meat, and I haven't been able to find it since they changed!

(73)   I'd better get Claire some Cheesits. She has asked for them the last three times I've come to the market. (There was a recording gap at this point, so her decision has been lost.)

(74)   Oh hey, I missed the frozen pies and I gotta go get those Jonny Mop "dealies." I gotta go back over there by the end of the meat counter. See, if that meat man had been here when I came, I wouldn't have got this fouled up.

(75)   You know, (laughter) I think they have moved them [the Jonny Mops] (laughter) or I'm thinking of another store. (At this point the interviewer displayed his absent-minded ignorance by failing to recognize the concept of a Jonny Mop and asked what it was.)

(76)   Oh, it's a Jonny Mop "dealy"—you know—for cleaning bathrooms.

INTERVIEWER:

(77)   Oh! (With an embarrassed red face at suddenly recognizing what the subject was talking about.)

SUBJECT:

(78)   I'd better buy some cookies. You know, for the

lunches. Usually I get those cup-custard things, but I've had 'em so many times, I'm kind of tired of 'em. I'll make some cookies this coming week. But—just—just, you know, for tomorrow. I got some pretty good fig bars down here the other day, if I can remember the brand I got. (Laughter.) Maybe I can recognize a package of 'em. (Laughter.) You know, they are in "dealy" and then there is two individual packs inside, and that way they stay fresher longer. I don't know if it came in a box, or a bag with a couple bags inside it.

(79)   You know, the way the store looks tonight, they probably don't have any. So I don't think we're blind, I think it's just that they are low on stock. (Laughter. The subject picked up another brand and commented on it.)

(80)   The dough looks so light on these, like it isn't baked. So—I like to have, uh—look like they have been baked a long time, you know, so that they are done, anyway. (The subject spent several minutes contemplating a purchase of this item.) Now, I'm so loused up I don't know which kind to buy.

(81)   You know, this old cart's getting a little heavy. You know what I think we're going to have to do? (Laughter.) I think we are going to need another one before we get out of here. (Chuckle. The interviewer attempted to help the subject find a cookie selection and suggested ginger snaps.)

(82)   But I don't like ginger snaps; I'm hungry for some fig newtons. Have you ever tried those peanut crunch cookies up there? They look like they might be good. Say—what are hermit cookies? (Laughter.) I'll go into hibernation if I'm going to have 'em. (Laughter.)

(83)   Oh hey! Here's a cookie—I'll get this one. These are good. They're just like candy. Chocolate peanut bars. Nope, changed my mind again!

INTERVIEWER:

(84)   Then you don't want the peanut crunches.

SUBJECT:

(85)   No, I don't want any peanut crunch, I'll get these Ideal chocolate peanut bars.

(86)   What aisle did we miss the cocoa in? You know, I don't know why they don't have the cocoa with the sugar, flour, and the chocolate. Stupid store, isn't it? (Laughter.)

(87)   Let's go this way, I need some soup—And if you see cocoa, holler!

(88)   Let's get some vegetable and Lipton's dry soup, and then I got to get some of this stuff up here—oh, uh— vegetable beef! (At this point, the subject and interviewer ran into each other as they tried to reach the soup. The temporary unbalance of both parties prompted the subject to say, (laughing) Let's have a little dance while we're looking. (When the interviewer expressed surprise, the subject quickly commented) You told me I could say anything that came to mind! (Hearty laughter.)

(89)   Here is the kind they like. Beef with vegetables and barley. Let me see—how many are there?—five for 89¢. O.K. Well, we'll get a couple cans of that, and—oh, maybe three of that, and then—and then, let's find some other that's five for 89¢.

(90)   See, I know what I'm doing, even if it doesn't seem like it. (Laughter.) Say, Bobby, would you like to do this every week? (Laughter.) Do you think we'll make it through the store on one tape? (Laughter.)

INTERVIEWER:

(91)   Do you want to select any from this group of soups that are five for 69¢?

SUBJECT:

(92)   No, that's five for 69¢ because it doesn't have any meat in it, see?

INTERVIEWER:

(93)   Oh, you're looking for something with meat in it?

SUBJECT:

(94)   So, it's gotta have—but—but the kind that are made with meat, then they are a little bit more. I'll get a couple of cans of that beef noodle. That's the same price.

(95)   Let's go up around the loop and see what's in the next aisle. I can't even remember.

(96)   Verna was kind of wrong—we haven't got the store all to ourselves, have we? (Verna is a neighbor who commented that at this hour on Sunday, no one would be in the store, so the subject probably wouldn't have cause for "mike fright.") Every once in a while I see someone looking. (Giggle. The subject then paused by the canned-vegetable section.) Oh, I was thinking of maybe getting some canned vegetables, but maybe they got something better in the frozen thing.

(97)   What kind of vegetable do you want Christmas Eve? (The interviewer and his wife had been invited to the subject's home for dinner on Christmas Eve.)

INTERVIEWER:

(98)   Oh, I don't know—

SUBJECT:

(99)   I thought you came to help! (Laughter.) You gotta do more than push the cart! (Hearty laughter.) Hey! Do you want to grab a couple of those Boston—the Heinz Boston-style beans in molasses sauce? Yeah—that's right. (The interviewer then asked her if she would like him to move her purse so more room could be made in the cart.)

(100)   I'll let my purse hang on my arm—I don't know—we gotta start on the bottom layer of this place, or shake this cart up.

INTERVIEWER:

(101)   Shall I get another cart?

SUBJECT:

(102)   Who's going to push it? (Laughter.) Oh! I need some Jell-O. Hey, that orange—have they had orange Jell-O before? Oh, yeah they have. Oh, they just got that in the big boxes. I haven't made this stuff for quite a while. That mixed fruit is pretty good—we'll get one of those, and I wish I remembered what my recipes called for. I wonder if I need some, uh—I think I need some raspberries. Three for 29¢, we gotta get another package of Jell-O!

(103)   Let's go down here by the season stuff—see right down here? (She looked at some salad mixes.) That's kind of good. Oh—this Italian salad, hey! That's got some good spices in it. That is good! Has Connie made any?

INTERVIEWER:

(104)   No, I don't think she has.

SUBJECT:

(105)   Hey! Look here! We found the cocoa! (Laughter.) Ah, you know, they think of it as a drink—I only think of it for baking. (It may be noted here that this situation reflects the nature of the classification problem associated with concept learning. More will be said about this in the text.)

(106)   What time is it? I see that mean man [the butcher she had returned the bad roast to on an earlier shopping trip] seems to be on duty. Shall I go order my round steak and my steaks? Hey! You hold this [the microphone] and I'll run down and check to see if they have put any in the meat case. (The subject checked with the meat man and found that they were all out of the cuts she wanted. However, they did give here a raincheck that allowed her to return and purchase the cuts at a later date but at today's special prices. This is a standing store policy. Here, comments on the incident follow, as she leaves the meat counter in search of the next items.)

(107)   Let's go down there, I know the canned fruit is over this way, and—I don't know, oh, let's—let's go up this aisle because if I get those steaks tomorrow—that meat man said they're all out of all the steak, and all he could offer me was sirloin tip, and that's 89¢ a pound against round steak at 69¢—and for what I want, the round steak is best. (She explained the raincheck to the interviewer.)

(108)   It's called a raincheck, see, so I can come down and get uh—what does that say? Has he got both kind of steaks on there?

INTERVIEWER:

(109)   It looks like—what was that, round steak? And what was the other you asked for?

SUBJECT:

(110)   I don't know—I asked for T-bone, but it doesn't look like he put T-bones down, does it? Oh, well. Well, I'd better get some A-1 Sauce 'cause I don't think we have much of that at home. Maybe that Kikko Man Sauce is in here. Boy, I don't know. I know where to find it up at Food Giant—no, that's Worcestershire. (Laughter at difficulty in pronouncing it.)

INTERVIEWER:

(111)   We must be close. It's meat sauce.

SUBJECT:

(112)   Yeah, but we gotta find soy sauces. I mean, regular soy sauce. Hey, maybe it's above the frozen food counter. They got spices over there, maybe they have it over there. We'll go back that way 'cause we gotta get that ice cream.

(113)   You know, if Jerry hears this tape, he's going to make me go to English class at night. (Laughter.)

(114)   Oh, I gotta go get a bag of potatoes again. We just got one bag, but, you know, if I'm going to make that Leftsa I'm going to have to have more potatoes. Oh—yeah, and we'll get some tomato juice. We're all out of that. So—oh boy.

(115)   I suppose you wonder why I'm smelling these potatoes, but you know, I've gotten potatoes, that, you know, they smell like a basement. And—oh gosh—you even taste that.

(116)   It would help if I knew what we were going to have Christmas Eve. Let's look at the frozen vegetables over here a minute. Maybe we can find something we want. (While the recorder was turned off, the subject asked the interviewer what vegetables he wanted for Christmas Eve dinner.)

INTERVIEWER:

(117)   Oh, most anything.

SUBJECT:

(118)   They don't have any "most anything," Bobby, you've gotta think of something else. (Hearty laughter. The interviewer then made a suggestion.)

(119)   You want me to make that dish of candied yams like I did at Thanksgiving? Oh, all right, then you can just help me pick out those yams! (Laughter.)

(120)   Now, we gotta go buy apples, too. (They are used in her recipe.) Here are the yams, kid! Here, I'll hold the bag and you just pick out—let's see—how many are we going to have for dinner that night? There's three of you, three of us, and mother—we need seven—oh, no. I'm going to make that casserole—Oh, just start piling 'em in and I'll tell you when to stop. Connie says the smallest ones are the best, aren't they?

INTERVIEWER:

(121)   I don't know. Seems to me she does say that.

SUBJECT:

(122)   Say, you know what? We went by that aisle where they have that rice and we forgot to get it for her. She isn't lucking out too well tonight is she? (Giggle.) Oh well, we can let them [the interviewer's wife and the subject's husband] go shopping tomorrow night and get what they want for Christmas Eve! (Very hearty laughter.)

(123)   No, the little ones [yams] aren't as stringy as the big ones, and I've got to slice them anyway for that casserole.

(124)   Do you want mashed potatoes and gravy that night? I'll be home all day, and you're coming over to help and so is Carlotta [interviewer's sister-in-law]. And there's Claire and Jerry and—Oh boy, we can have a good dinner. You know, on a pork roast, we'll get a real good gravy. So shall we have some mashed potatoes and gravy?

INTERVIEWER:

(125)   Yeah.

SUBJECT:

(126)   Oh oh! I didn't say stop [putting yams in the bag]! You can stop now. (The interviewer asked if she wanted to put any back.) No, we'll take 'em all. I'll bet the people watching think we've had a few too many! (Laughter.) Yeah, otherwise we wouldn't have been able to get this far! (Laughter.)

(127)   Here's the tomato juice. Oh, they're all the same price, so let's take Libby's. I'll try not to drop 'em this time. (Giggle.)

(128)   I've gotta go over and get some of these tangerines. They're on sale. And then we'll stop up there and see if we can find some wine-sap apples. (The interviewer started to weigh the tangerines.)

(129)   Gee, they will weigh 'em at the check-out stand, Bobby. (Giggle.)

INTERVIEWER:

(130)   Oh, then you don't weigh 'em. You just pick out as many as you feel you need?

(131)   Yeah, I just pick out as many as I want, and uh—they're only two pounds for 29¢—oh hey! We gotta get some, uh—Oh, I don't know what kind of salad I'm making, so we'll get some mandarin oranges, and uh,—I guess they don't make this one in low-calorie stuff, but I

gotta get some of that fruit cocktail in the low-cal department. Here—Dole has it. There is another one, too. Some Delight product that's low calorie, but I can't find it. So, I should get some uh—I think I'll get some cranberries, and I'd better get a couple cans of oranges. I'll make a couple salads with oranges in them.

(132)   Hey, I wonder if this Cherry Star brand is any good, or if I'd better get Del Monte like I usually do. Uh, I might as well be a sport and try a different brand, I've never had it before though. Yeah, we'll try two cans of that [Cherry Star brand of oranges]. We'll be real brave tonight.

(133)   Better push this cart gently, if one of those cans falls on your toe, you'll be screaming! (Giggle.)

(134)   Oh, and I need a can of whole-berry cranberry sauce, I wonder what—oh, and I'd better get a can of pineapple tid-bits. Back up! (We went back for the pineapple she had forgotten in this aisle.) Oh, we missed this way down at the end of this aisle. (Laughter.) Oh, I only need one can of that.

(135)   Now, if we get those apples, we'll have the sweet-potato casserole, won't we? I can't remember what else went in it. I'll probably have to come back down before Christmas, anyway. You can come with me again, if you want. I like help pushing the basket. (Laughter. We continued on for the next item.)

(136)   Hold it! You're going past the wine-saps. I'll just get three, because I don't think it took very many.

(137)   You know, I think I'll go home and rebuild my lunch. (She makes it the night before.) I don't think I've got enough for work tomorrow. I'm getting awfully hungry in this store!

(138)   Oops! I just stubbed my toe. I'm not dancing. (Giggle.)

(139)   They've got Simple Simon Pies on sale, so let's go down this aisle and get some.

(140)   Oh, oh, traffic jam! Guess we'll just have to wait it out. (Laughter. We then started down the crowded aisle.)

(141)   Look out, Bobby, you're going to crash! (Laughter.) I guess you scared her out! (Laughter, as the interviewer suddenly stopped and backed up to keep from hitting a lady in front of him.)

(142)   Hey! That's my toe you're running over! (Laughter.) Let's turn around. I don't think we'll ever get through.

(143)   We're in the wrong aisle again, we've gotta go around the bend. Here we got frozen dinners, and we want frozen pies. To the right. Yeah. Do you see that fellow looking at us? (Laughter.) I'm going to get the giggles so bad, I'll never get through the check-out stand. (Laughter. We then found the pies and the interviewer picked up a pie.)

(144)   Yeah, but that's Morton's, and we need Simple Simon. Simple pies for simple people! (Laughter.)

(145)   I think I'll get a boysenberry pie. They're kind of good.

(146)   I'm going to feed you an apple when we get home—a piece of apple pie, that is. Not an apple. I'm going to save those apples you know, I need for Christmas Eve dinner.

(147)   How about if we find that curried rice for Connie? And I've still got to look above the frozen counter where the spices are for that Kikko Man Sauce.

INTERVIEWER:

(148)   Say, you didn't forget!

SUBJECT:

(149)   Sure, I've got a one-track mind. I don't forget! (We continued to that section of the store).

(150)   I bet we found it [the rice and the Kikko Man Sauce]. Here's the Chinese food. I'll bet we find it down here. Hey! I'm getting ahead of ya. (The subject walked up to the spice section.)

(151)   There is Kikko Man Sauce! Shall I get her a big bottle or a little bottle?

INTERVIEWER:

(152)   How much does it take?

SUBJECT:

(153)   It doesn't take too much. I don't know if she will use it in other things—it keeps a long time, though, and I use a lot of it. You know, that's what I did the chicken in tonight. And you can do chuck steaks, and barbecue 'em, and it's real good. You can put it on just—just anything. It isn't very good on ice cream though.

INTERVIEWER:

(154)   Oh, have you tried it?

SUBJECT:

(155)   I have not tried it, it just came through my mind. (Laughter.) You told me I could say whatever came to mind. (Giggle.) You don't know what circles *my* mind goes in! (Laughter.)

(156)   Here, how about some confetti? We can get ready for New Year's. (Laughter.) Pass that up.

(157)   I think the rice [she was to get for Connie] should be over in that next aisle, so if I pick up those ice-cream bars now, you can go up to the check-out stand. Say, I'd better get some vanilla in a carton, too, some of that Jersey Maid, because we may want some on our pie. I'm getting awfully hungry! (The interviewer reached for the vanilla carton for the subject.) That's ice milk, Bobby. I want ice cream.

INTERVIEWER:

(158)   Oops! I didn't notice. Say, is there much of a difference?

SUBJECT:

(159)   Sure, I want this Jersey Maid. It's got more calories. When I have something sweet, I want it real sweet, you know, for dessert. (We then went to find the rice on our way to the check-stand.)

(160)   Here, hold the basket and I'll run [down this aisle] and look [for the rice]. I see it way over back there towards the fruit department—I see macaroni. Do you suppose we can find rice in there? (We approached the area she had spotted.)

(161)   Hold it! Let's go down here to the left. You know, usually there's a lot of fellows wandering around here. They don't even seem to be stocking the shelves tonight. You know, then you can ask 'em where the stuff is instead of running all over looking.

(162)   What was that stuff she wanted now?

INTERVIEWER:

(163)   Oh, it was curried rice.

SUBJECT:

(164)   She said it came in a—yeah, but she said it came in a bag. That's in a box. Let's just look for a bag. Anything we see in a bag, we'll take it home. (Laughter.)

(165)   You know, I've seen those—I think up at another market they had, uh—you know, more of a variety than that. They had some in bags, you know, like this, regular rice, but I don't see any here.

(166)   Let's see, macaroni, spaghetti Italiano, Rice-a-Roni —Hey! There's those bags of rice. Let's see if we can find it up here. Well, what do you know—we finally found it in a bag! Think we should buy the whole box of bags after all this? (Chuckle.)

INTERVIEWER:

(167)   (Chuckle.) I don't think she wanted but one.

SUBJECT:

(168)   Let's check out and see if I've got enough money now. Be funny if we have to go start putting all this back! (Hearty laughter.) Maybe you'll have to foot me a small loan. (More chuckles.)

(169)   Shall we look at the list and see what I missed?

INTERVIEWER:

(170)   Let's see, did I have that in my pocket?

SUBJECT:

(171)   It doesn't do me any good in your pocket, or did you lose it?

INTERVIEWER:

(172)   Gee, I don't have the list. I gave it back to you!

SUBJECT:

(173)   But you took it, no, that's my raincheck on the meat, but you took my list. No, that's not it (as the interviewer took something from his pocket), that's your letter. You probably—oh, here's my coupon—Oh! I gotta go pick up my free glass, 'cause I got over five dollars worth of stuff here. I must have about $35.00. (The actual bill came to $32.20. Some interesting comments will be made about this factor in the text. The list was found and the subject reviewed it.)

(174)   Oh, I still didn't get the Jonny-Mops. I'll just look for those when I come back for the meat tomorrow. I'm ready to go home.

An Analysis of the Shopping Process

This section represents an attempt by the author to hypothesize a flow diagram that could be used as a model for simulating the behavior of a typical shopper. An effort has been made in constructing this diagram to reflect all the actions taken by the subject during the shopping tour in which her protocol was obtained. An overview of this flow diagram will first be given, followed by a more detailed explanation of the diagram as related to certain specific actions the subject was observed to take. During this second phase of the explanation, reference will be made to the numbered paragraphs of the preceding protocol.

An Overview of the Model

The flow diagram in Figure A-1 shows that the process is begun by inputting data describing the subject's basic history,

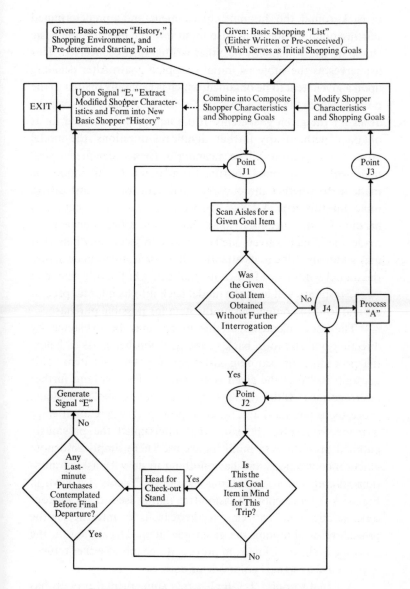

FIGURE A-1. Simulation Model, Flow Diagram.

or background, the shopping environment, and a predetermined starting point for the tour. Also input into the model is the basic shopping list, which may be either written or preconceived. This list serves as the subject's initial shopping goals. After deciding upon a given item to be obtained, which is generally related to the point at which the tour is to start, the model proceeds to scan the aisles for the given goal items. If the item being searched for is obtained without any further significant questions, the model advances to point J-2. The meaning of *further significant questions* will be explained shortly. From point J-2 an inquiry is made as to whether the previous goal item was the last one in mind for this trip. A "Yes" answer will lead to an action of heading for the check-out stand. But before a final departure is made, the model is given one last chance to secure any item that may suddenly come to its attention. If no such situation develops, the model will proceed on to its final exit. On the other hand, a "Yes" response will loop the model back into its internal processes and lead to contemplating the item for possible purchase.

The other elements of this model may be explained by directing our attention back to the question being asked below the procedure of scanning aisles for a given goal item. This question is, "Was the given goal item obtained without further interrogation?" If the answer to this question is "No," the model proceeds to point J-4 and hence to process A, where an attempt is made to resolve the issue that interrupted the previously outlined procedure. (J numbers are used here simply to denote junction connections and have nothing to do with asking questions, taking action, or making decisions.) Process A, shown in Figure A-2, represents a decision tree that is used to ask all conceivable questions that relate to the reasons for interrupting the procedure of obtaining the given goal item. Depending on the outcome of the decision from process A, the model either returns to point J-2 or signals point J-3, or both.

A signal to point J-3 implies that some mental process has occurred that will serve to modify the shopper's characteristics and/or shopping goal. In other words, the experience encountered by the model that led to process A will leave the shopper in a different state from that which obtained prior to an encounter with this experience and must be incorporated into the composite shopper characteristics and goals as a new element of learned experience. A signal to point J-3 places the simulated shopper into the new state by modifying his characteristics and shopping goals.

The question asked below point J-2, "Is this the last goal item in mind for this trip?" has a "No" branch that returns the model to point J-1. The indicated recursive mode thus continues until the model has exhaustively explored all purchase decisions in mind for the present trip.

The generation of signal E signifies that the present shopping tour has been definitely completed and that the simulated shopper is ready to exit from the model. As previously noted, however, it is highly improbable that the shopper would exit in the same state as that in which he entered. In recognition of this fact, the final procedure used in the model is to extract the modified shopper characteristics and form these factors into a new set of basic shopper history. Thus the knowledge, experience, and attitudes that have been modified by interaction with the existing shopping environment now form a part of the new total history with which the shopper will approach his next shopping task.

A More Detailed Description of the Model

The upper left-hand block in Figure A-1 shows the given input factors to the model to be (1) The basic shopper history, (2) the shopping environment, and (3) the predetermined starting point.

The data describing basic shopper history must be sufficient to convey an extremely large quantity of information. Included in this category are all those elements of shopper experience and status that, either directly or indirectly, influence his ability to make the needed decisions within the given shopping environment.

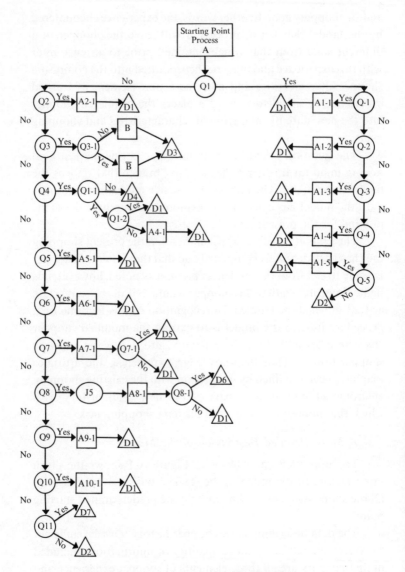

FIGURE A-2. Process "A" Decision Tree.

Explanation of Process *A* Decision Tree (FIGURE A-2)

Is further interrogation required because

*Q*1   the price, brand, quantity, packaging, or any combination thereof is in question?

    (*Q*1-1)   Is the price in question?

        (*A*1-1)   Apply shopper's price standards and decide to buy or not to buy.

            (*D*1)   Signal *J*-3 to modify shopper characteristics and return to *J*-2.

    (*Q*1-2)   Is the brand in question?

        (*A*1-2)   Apply shopper's brand knowledge and decide to buy or not to buy.

            (*D*1)   Signal *J*-3 to modify shopper characteristics and return to *J*-2.

    (*Q*1-3)   Is the quantity in question?

        (*A*1-3)   Apply shopper's quantity requirements and decide to buy or not to buy.

            (*D*1)   Signal *J*-3 to modify shopper characteristics and return to *J*-2.

    (*Q*1-4)   Is the packaging in question?

        (*A*1-4)   Apply shopper's knowledge and/or bias concerning package requirements and decide to buy or not to buy.

            (*D*1)   Signal *J*-3 to modify shopper characteristics and return to *J*-2.

    (*Q*1-5)   Is any combination of *Q*1-1 through *Q*1-4 in question?

        (*A*1-5)   Interrelate all relevant factors and decide to buy or not to buy.

            (*D*1)   Signal *J*-3 to modify shopper characteristics and return to *J*-2.

            (*D*2)   Arrival at this point indicates a logic error and generates an ERROR-HALT signal.

*Q*2   the ingredients are in question?

    (*A*2-1)   Apply shopper's knowledge, standards, and requirements concerning ingredients and decide to buy or not to buy.

        (*D*1)   Signal *J*-3 to modify shopper characteristics and return to *J*-2.

*Q*3   the item is the last one and is damaged somehow?

(Q3-1)   Does the damage matter in this instance?
   (B)   If no to Q3-1, buy.
   (B)   If yes to Q3-1, don't buy.
   (D3)   Return to J-2.
   (D4)   If no to Q4-1, decide to resolve the issue later and return to J-2.

Q4   the item dosen't seem to be in its usual location?
   (Q4-1)   Is the issue important enough to resolve now?
      (D4)   If no to Q4-1, decide to resolve the issue later and return to J-2.
   (Q4-2)   Has it been definitely determined that the shopping environment does not contain the item?
      (D1)   Signal J-3 to modify shopper characteristics and return to J-2.
   (A4-1)   Take required action to discover status of this item, and make decision to buy or not to buy.
      (D1)   Signal J-3 to modify shopper characteristics and return to J-2.

Q5   another previously decided-upon item has been found unexpectedly?
   (A5-1)   Apply shopper's knowledge, standards, and requirements concerning this item and decide to buy or not to buy.
      (D1)   Signal J-3 to modify shopper characteristics and return to J-2.

Q6   a question has arisen as to whether this kind of item is actually wanted?
   (A6-1)   Review relevant factors concerning the original decision to buy this item and make decision to buy or not to buy.
      (D1)   Signal J-3 to modify shopper characteristics and return to J-2.

Q7   it has been temporarily forgotten what item is being searched for?
   (A7-1)   Review shopper characteristics in an effort to recall item.
   (Q7-1)   Was recall process successful?
      (D5)   If yes to Q7-1, continue to search for item.
      (D1)   If no to Q7-1, signal J-3 to modify shopper characteristics and return to J-2.

Q8   some happenchance called attention to a previously unthought-of item that may be needed?

(*A*8-1) Consult shopper knowledge, standards, and requirements concerning this item and decide to buy or not to buy.
Does this item call attention to some other item that may be needed?

(*D*1) If no to *Q*8-1, signal *J*-3 to modify shopper characteristics and return to *J*-2.

(*D*6) If yes to *Q*8-1, return to *J*-5 and follow recursive procedure until a no is given to *Q*8-1.

*Q*9 some happenchance aroused curiosity concerning an item not presently needed but about which background information could be obtained?

(*A*9-1) Compile the desired background data.

(*D*1) Signal *J*-3 to modify shopper characteristics and return to *J*-2.

*Q*10 some situation has developed in which several of the above questions need to be explored simultaneously?

(*A*10-1) Apply shopper's logic to interrelate the relevant variables and make a decision to buy or not to buy.

(*D*1) Signal *J*-3 to modify shopper characteristics and return to *J*-2.

*Q*11 some situation has developed in which the preceding questions, of themselves, are insufficient to resolve the issue?

(*D*2) Arrival at this point indicates a logic error and generates an ERROR-HALT signal.

(*D*7) Arrival at this point indicates that the system has not been designed to cover all contingencies, and alerts the operator to have the system design evaluated.

This data would include, for example, the preconceived attitudes, knowledge, and rules with which the shopper is armed to make purchasing decisions for any item he may encounter. It also includes the status of his present and anticipated future economic positions. No imagination is required to recognize that this factor alone can have a major and direct influence upon all the shopper's decisions. Without laboring the point, one only needs to recognize that all shopping decisions made during the tour will be influenced by the present state of the total background, or history, possessed by the shopper as he enters the shopping environment.

The second item input into the model is sufficient data with which to describe fully the shopping environment in which the tour will be conducted. This data, for example, must describe in sufficient detail each and every item contained within this environment. Data of this nature must describe the classification of items available, the different brands of each item classification, the quantity and packaging factors of each item, the price of each item, the relative location of each item, and possibly many other factors the author has not thought of at the moment.

The last item of this input information is the logical starting point for the tour. This point would be based upon the shopper's knowledge of the environment's total layout.

The upper right-hand block in Figure A-1 indicates the second given input factor to be the basic shopping list, which serves as the initial shopping goals. This list may be either written or preconceived. Although most shoppers will approach the shopping tour with a written list, it has been discovered that a large number of items are hold in memory without being translated into written form. These goals serve only as an initial standard for the shopper, because it has been observed that numerous items are both added and deleted from this initial list as the shopper gains experience through interaction with the shopping environment. It will be found, for example, that the shopper may add an impulse item to his purchases when confronted by the opportunity. On the other hand, a change in plans for making a certain recipe may cause the shopper to delete several items from the basic list. Suffice it to say that innumerable circumstances may cause the ultimate purchases to differ radically from the initial goals.

The given factors from both blocks are next combined into a composite set of shopper characteristics and shopping goals. This composite picture represents the initial state in which the shopper enters the shopping environment. As noted in the overview description, the aisles are then scanned for a given goal item. If this item is obtained without further interrogation, the tour will proceed to point *J*-2. The phrase *without further interrogation* is intended to imply that the shopper located the goal item without directing his attention to any mental activity other than that of finding the exact item he had in mind, ascertaining that the price, quantity, brand, and packaging met his expectations and thus made the purchase. Further interrogations refer to any activities that fall outside this definition.

An example related to the preceding protocol may serve to illustrate this point. In paragraph 2, the subject first decided to go to the meat department and obtain several specific items. But an examination of the meat case disclosed that her goal items were apparently unavailable. For this reason, the subject decided to ring the bell and have the butcher produce the desired items. In the model of Figure A-1, this is equivalent to a signal for entering process *A*. The analogy may be continued from this point by tracing Figure A-2 to the appropriate question reflecting these circumstances.

By observing the explanations attached to the decision tree for process *A* (Figure A-2), the reader will find that the series of questions being asked here will ultimately direct him to question $Q4$. These explanations begin by asking, "Is further interrogation required because ($Q1$) the price, brand, quantity, packaging, or any combination thereof is in question?" A sequential reading of these questions will result in question $Q4$ which asks, in essence, "Is further interrogation required because the item does not seem to be in its usual location?" This is the situation reflected in paragraph 2 of the protocol. Returning once again to the explanations, the reader will find question $Q4$-1 asks, "Is the issue important enough to resolve now?" The subject's affirmative answer to this question leads her to ask question $Q4$-2, "Has it been definitely determined that the shopping environment does not contain the item?" The "No" answer to this question leads her to take action A4-1, which is an attempt to discover the status of this item and make a decision to buy or not to buy. But failure to resolve this issue—because the meatman was off duty—leaves her no alternative but to take action D1. When she takes action D1, the shopper characteristics are modified to reflect the fact that this goal item was unobtained and must be searched for a second time. Meanwhile, however, the shopper is directed to point J-2 and placed back in the touring loop.

A few more examples will be given in order to familiarize the reader with the use of the simulation model. But these examples may serve a larger purpose than simply gaining this familiarity, for nearly all the subject's interactions with the shopping environment carry hidden clues to the nature of cognitive processes. Because of this, many of these examples will be accompanied by remarks that reflect the insight one may gain through an interrelation of the protocol with the simulation model.

It will be observed in paragraph 102 of the protocol that the subject had been contemplating the purchase of Jell-O when, by happenchance, she spotted a display of mixed fruits. This is equivalent to a situation in which the simulation model enters process A in response to question Q8, "Has some happenchance called attention to a previously unthought-of item that may be needed?" Question Q8 leads through point J-5 to activity A8-1, "Consult shopper's knowledge, standards, and requirements concerning this item and decide to buy or not to buy." In the present instance, the subject decided that the mixed fruit met her requirements and made a purchase. But the circumstances surrounding this purchase caused her to ponder the purchase of some raspberries. This action is equivalent to a "Yes" answer to question Q8-1, which asks, "Does this item call attention to some other item that may be needed?" Having obtained a "Yes" answer, the model is instructed to make decision D6, which states, "If 'Yes' to Q8-1, return to J-5 and follow recursive procedure until a 'No' answer is given to Q8-1." In returning to point J-5, the model is directed to again take action A8-1, i.e., "consult shopper's knowledge, standards, and requirements concerning this item and decide to buy or not to buy." Once this decision has been made, the model again asks question $Q8-1$, in search of a "No" answer. It is seen from the protocol that when the subject obtained her "No" answer, she returned to her normal shopping procedures, which in our model is analogous to leaving process A and returning to point J-2.

This encounter may also provide some hidden clues for the systems designer who would attempt to simulate the preceding cognitive processes. As noticed from paragraph 102, the subject found herself uncertain about which items were needed because she could not fully remember what her recipes called for. How will the model builder simulate this characteristic of human behavior?

Digital computer programs are generally written to handle discrete bits of data that are stored in precisely known memory locations. (Even though advanced programming techniques often allow the programmer to use such methods as symbolic addressing, the idea is that the system itself is designed to keep track of its memory data and can obtain them as needed.) The binary nature of these bits further implies that the meaning of the symbol they represent is either completely accurate or totally wrong. Thus the computer has either total recall or no recall concerning the various elements of data within its memory.

Such is not the case with the human being, for his data are available from memory in varying degrees of intensity and accuracy. He may find, for example, that a given element of desired information somehow escapes him. Although he may not be able to recall this information in total, he is often bothered by the notion that it is "just around the corner." Quite frequently, the human being may be able to reconstruct the missing data by directing his thoughts to historical circumstances surrounding the subject in question. In short, the human being's total history of background information frequently allows him to synthesize, or locate, forgotten data by using certain characteristics of his cognitive processes. This phenomenon could be looked at in two different ways.

On the one hand, it could be argued that the cells containing the data had actually become disarranged but that the human mind was able to reconstruct the information by applying the logical processes of inductive and/or deductive reasoning. For example, we have all had the experience of trying to recall something by saying, "Since this was true and that was true, it therefore follows that—." In this manner, we often arrive at the information we need but, even then, cannot verify with certainty that present facts are as we originally conceived them. All we can say is that the logic of the situation implies that "it must have been this way."

On the other hand, it could be argued that the missing information was still contained within the brain cells but that the conscious mind had lost track of the search path required to bring these data into focus. This view holds that the phenomenon is simply a problem of memory organization and that information later recalled has resulted from the application of an association search process. For example, each of us can recall saying something to ourselves like the following, "Now let's see. I was standing on the corner waiting for the light to turn green when it started raining. But I had just left the restaurant and gone to the drugstore for some cigarettes when I ran into Bill and—That's it! I left my raincoat on the door hook of the washroom at the restaurant, because I didn't have anything in my hands when I talked to Bill. I can see it hanging there now."

But whatever the reason, the fact still remains that the capacity for this phenomenon must be simulated by any model that purports to produce decisions that parallel its human counterpart. Consideration of the preceding factors is at least sufficient to establish that the human cognitive processes are not wholly of a digital nature but appear, rather, to be a combination of both digital and analog elements. These phenomena give rise to a strong suspicion that successful models for simulating cognitive processes should contain a combination of both digital and analog characteristics. In short, the model builder must somehow find a way to simulate this human weakness, or he may find that the computer's total-recall capacity will defeat his purpose.

Paragraph 22 may be used to illustrate the manner in which the model absorbs background information concerning its environment even though there is no immediate need for this knowledge. It is observed that the subject found herself contemplating a box of "man-sized tissues" while in the process of making a needed purchase. There was no serious effort made to acquire this product, for her protocol shows her to have already made her decision. But this situation is reflected in the model by question $Q9$, which asks, "Has some happenchance aroused curiosity concerning an item not presently needed but about which background information could be obtained?" An affirmative answer to question $Q9$ leads to action $A9$-1, i.e., to compiling the desired background data. Once this is done, the decision $D1$ signals point J-3 to modify the shopper's characteristics by incorporating this information as a new element of learned experience. The model is then returned to its normal search path through point J-2.

Another example of the model's operation can be given in connection with paragraph 72. We see here that the subject had selected a goal item of "something for sandwiches." If is furthermore seen that she had tentatively decided upon Oscar Meyer's Thuringer as the particular brand and type of goal item. But something happened to prevent her from obtaining this item without further interrogations. When it was discovered that the shopping environment apparently did not contain the brand and type of goal item in mind, the subject's attention was directed toward obtaining some substitute. She ultimately made a purchase of all-meat summer sausage and took note that her experience in this interaction with the shopping environment had failed to remedy the difficulties that she had been having with finding this item since its manufacturer changed his packaging techniques.

These actions are simulated in the model by several questions. The preceding situation corresponds to question $Q10$ of the protocol, which asks, "Has some situation developed in which several of the preceding questions need to be explored simultaneously?" Since the answer to this question is "Yes," the model proceeds to take action $A10$-1, which is to apply the shopper's logic to interrelate the relevant variables and make a decision to buy or not to buy. The interrelation of these relevant variables takes place as follows: First of all, the fact that the desired goal item was not found in its usual location calls for question $Q4$. The "Yes" answer to question $Q4$ directs the model to question $Q4$-1, which asks, "Is the issue important enough to resolve now?" The subject's affirmative answer to this question directs the model to question $Q4$-2, which asks, "Has it been definitely determined that the shopping environment does not contain the item?" Her "No" answer to this question leads to action $A4$-1, which is to take the required action to discover the status of this item. The subject's action in this case was to study the meat counter in enough detail to decide for herself that the item was not available. And here is where the several questions begin to be explored simultaneously. While in the process of trying to ascertain the status of the desired item, the subject happened to spot the all-meat summer sausage, which she thought might satisfy her needs. This action calls forth question $Q8$ in the model. It asks, "Has some happenchance called attention to a previously unthought-of item that might be needed?" The "Yes" answer then causes action $A8$-1 to occur, in which the shopper consults her knowledge, standards, and requirements concerning the all-meat summer sausage and makes the decision to buy. Since in this instance the next question, $Q8$-1 receives a "No" answer (because this particular situation did not call attention to any other item that might be needed), the model proceeds to decision $D1$, where a signal is applied to point J-3 to modify the shopper's characteristics. In this instance, the characteristic modified was simply that of noting the still continuing failure to identify a desired goal item with the new packaging methods its producer had employed. The model is then returned to point J-2.

A final example for this section of the report will be given to show how the model handles a different type of situation.

Prior to paragraph 105 of the protocol, the subject had made several attempts to locate the goal item "cocoa." Although she had not verbalized her desire for this item previously, paragraph 86 indicates that this item had been in question several times, for at that point she stated, "What aisle did we miss the cocoa in? You know, I don't know why they don't have that cocoa with the sugar, flour, and the chocolate. Stupid store, isn't it?" The shopping tour continued until paragraph 105, at which point the subject commented, "Hey! Look here! We found the cocoa! Ah, you know, they think of it as a drink—I only think of it for baking."

This incident is reflected in the model by question $Q5$, which asks, "Is further interrogation required because another previously decided-upon item has been found unexpectedly?" The "Yes" answer to this question leads the model to action $A5$-1, where the subject applies her knowledge, standards, and requirements concerning this item and makes the decision to buy. Exit from this path is made through decision $D1$, where signal J-3 is applied to modify the shopper's characteristics before returning to point J-2. And herein lies a very significant clue for getting a handle on the computer-simulation problem. The subject's statement that "they think of it as a drink—I only think of it for baking," reflects the nature of the classification problem. In a sense, the subject of our protocol has formed a new concept by absorbing the object "drink" into the classification for the name "cocoa," whereas her original classification rules had only included the object "food."

The final remarks of this section will serve to acquaint the reader with a rather curious factor noticed by the author in this protocol. In paragraph 173 the subject concluded her tour by remarking, "Oh! I gotta go pick up my free glass, 'cause I got over five dollars worth of stuff here. I must have about $35.00." The bill actually came to $32.20. It strikes the author as curious that the subject, while not at all consciously totaling her purchases as she proceeded, was able to guess the total within 10 per cent of its actual value. And the spontaneous manner in which she made this statement shows that she had taken no appreciable time to contemplate the entire marketing tour. In light of these facts, one cannot help but wonder what characteristics of the human mind could be responsible for this degree of calculating ability. But these are questions that cannot be answered until we have learned a great deal more about the human thought processes.

Suggested Goals for Future Study

To this point, the paper has attempted to outline the problem involved in attempting to simulate the cognitive processes of the human shopper as he fills his basket with items from a supermarket. The basis for the study has consisted of a taped protocol taken during an actual shopping experience, and this protocol has been analyzed and reduced to an initial flow diagram of the processes involved. Several questions have been asked of this protocol in order to ascertain the nature of the work that is yet to be done before a running computer program may be designed. At this point we shall ask what direction future studies may take.

It is noted that the ultimate goal of creating a computer program in which the human shopper can be completely simulated is, indeed, quite far in the future. If such a program could be implemented, it would imply that a number of tasks had been successfully achieved.

For one thing, it would imply that we had been successful in finding ways to extract the huge quantity of historical information that a subject acquires through a lifetime of experiences. It would also imply that we had been successful in discovering the many variable, and often illogical, processing rules that a given human being uses in a wide variety of situations. Consider these statements for a moment. The modern supermarket contains literally thousands of different items—possibly between fifteen and twenty thousand items. A human subject enters this shopping environment with a preconceived notion of what he is after. This notion has usually been established on the basis of his most recent needs. But once he is confronted by this environment, there can be but little question that his various decisions reflect the sum total of all knowledge he has acquired to date.

Before any simulation model could hope to predict, with accuracy, the decisions this shopper will make in this complex, although bounded, environment, the model would have to have been programmed to know the subject's decision rules for every conceivable item classification that lay before him. It would have to know the illogical as well as the logical processes of these rules and apply them on the same basis as its human counterpart. It would also have to know the sum total of all factors surrounding the daily living experiences of the subject. The model could not hope, for example, to predict the decision to buy a chicken for Sunday dinner because Aunt Mary is coming, unless it had been specifically told that this was a significant factor in the subject's living pattern.

For another thing, the sheer volume of statistical data collection concerning the shopping environment of the typical supermarket may make it both discouraging as well as impractical to specify the shopping environment in the details required to simulate precisely the experiences encountered in a real-life situation. One must consider that specification of this environment would have to include not only every classification of every item available but also every brand, price, quantity, size, location, and many other factors too numerous to list at this point. But viewing this ultimate version of the simulation process should not discourage further study, nor lead one to conclude that further study would be futile. There are ways in which this problem can be attacked, and its undertaking could prove quite fruitful for shedding light on subjects in the field of psychology as well as computer science.

The magnitude of this problem could be considerably scaled down in order to gain a starting point. It would be possible, for example, to restrict the objective of the initial simulation model to that of simulating the shopper's choices from a limited list of known item classifications. The researcher could begin by asking the subject to list the kind of food items to be selected during a given shopping tour, and then go over this restricted list with the subject in an attempt to learn the decision rules she normally applies to selecting items within these classifications. If this interview were conducted with the proper thought and care, sufficient knowledge might be obtained with which to construct a very simple, although limited, model of the shopper's characteristics that are influential within these categories. Since the goal requirements would be restricted, the shopping environment would need only to include the specification of item classifications that could possibly fulfill these goals. Such a list may not be too difficult to obtain from inventory records of the given supermarket in which the tour would be conducted. At any rate, the objective would simply be an attempt to predict the shopper's reactions to a known environment for a limited number of known goal items. Whatever else the shopper did during the shopping period would be irrelevant for this comparison.

In this manner, the researcher, working with the same subject over a period of time, would be able to accumulate an historical background that would more accurately characterize the shopper with each new shopping experience. And if the experiments were conducted in the same supermarket each time, it would be possible to slowly build a history of the shopping environment. But no conjecture will be made by the author as to how far this process may usefully go.

When one reflects on the magnitude of the problems involved in attempting to construct the ultimate version of the shopper simulation model, he can readily appreciate why Newell and Simon[6] restricted the study of their General Problem Solver to the task of having their subject attack his problem with a limited and well-defined set of mathematical rules, and why Clarkson was able to simulate the decisions of an investment trust officer. In the first case, Newell and Simon allowed their subject to use only twelve mathematical logic expressions that, if properly manipulated, would yield an exact solution to his problem. In the case of Clarkson's investment trust model, it is recognized that, although there is a relatively large number of investment parameters that one could consider, the goals for investment can be rather easily stated in terms of mathematical relations and symbols. Also, the nature of investments is such that a large background of historical data is readily available for specifying the task environment. These situations are quite different from that which describes the shopper simulation problem.

In conclusion, it is noted that the importance of this topic for further research study is not to be found in whether the ultimate simulation is ever achieved, for its true value would simply lie in the usefulness of the knowledge that may be obtained along the way to this goal.

6. A. Newell and H. Simon, "GPS, A Program that Simulates Human Thought," in Feigenbaum and Feldman, *op. cit.*

Chapter 2

An Introduction to Adaptive Models of Consumer Behavior

The idea that consumers are capable of adaptive behavior is a common one that underlies much recent work aimed at providing a theoretical description of consumer behavior.[1]

These two rules of thumb (learning and utility maximization) are related to a certain extent, as has been briefly mentioned in Chapter 1. However, they also lead to quite different results since the first tends to focus attention on short-run aspects of behavior and the second to focus attention on long-run aspects of behavior.

This chapter provides an introduction to the types of theories that arise when the capability for adaptive behavior is

---

1. A. A. Kuehn, "Mathematical Models of Consumer Behavior," in Joseph W. Newman, ed., *On Knowing the Consumer*, John Wiley & Sons, Inc., New York, 1966, p. 495. I am indebted to Dan Braunstein, Douglas Dalrymple, and Alvin J. Silk for comments on draft versions of this chapter. All customary disclaimers apply.

assumed. Specific results, discussion of examples, and empirical results are deferred, in general, to later chapters.[2]

Introduction

Historically, the most popular theory of consumer behavior that exhibits simple adaptive properties has been the first-order Markov chain.[3] The essence of the first-order Markov chain may be simply described. Suppose there are three states of the world, S_1, S_2, and S_3, each of which represent purchasing a particular brand of a consumer nondurable in a given time period. The purchase sequence of a consumer may be described, it is postulated. by the following transition matrix:

To

$$\begin{array}{ccc} S_1 & S_2 & S_3 \end{array}$$

$$S_1$$

From $S_2 \quad [p_{ij}]$ (2-1)

$$S_3$$

S_1, S_2, and S_3 are the three possible states, and p_{ij} is the probability of going from state i to state j. In this formulation,

2. Previous introductory and/or review articles on this subject are Jerome D. Herniter and Ronald A. Howard, "Stochastic Marketing Models," in *Progress In Operations Research*, vol. 2, John Wiley & Sons, Inc., New York, 1963; Jerome D. Herniter, "Stochastic Market Models and the Analysis of Consumer Panel Data," in *American Chemical Society (Division of Chemical Marketing and Economics), Symposia on General Rubber Chemicals and Marketing Economics; Purchase and Exchange of Technical Know-How; Mathematical Models in Chemical Marketing*, American Chemical Society, New York, 1966; David B. Montgomery, "Stochastic Modeling of the Consumer," *Industrial Management Review*, vol. 8, no. 2, Spring, 1967.

3. One of the earliest discussions of this theoretical approach is found in Richard B. Maffei, "Brand Preferences and Simple Markov Processes," *Operations Research*, vol. 8, no. 2, March-April, 1960, pp. 210–218. This article has been reprinted in B. M. Bass, et al., *Mathematical Models and Methods in Marketing*, Richard D. Irwin, Inc., Homewood, Illinois, 1961, pp. 109–118.

the rows of the P matrix must sum to one (i.e., each row can be thought of as a probability vector). For example,

$$(1 \quad 0 \quad 0) \quad \begin{matrix} \frac{1}{2} & \frac{1}{4} & \frac{1}{4} \\ \frac{1}{2} & 0 & \frac{1}{2} \\ \frac{1}{2} & \frac{1}{4} & \frac{1}{2} \end{matrix} = (\frac{1}{2} \quad \frac{1}{4} \quad \frac{1}{4}).$$

Symbolically, $S_0 P = S_1$. P is a constant, and S_0 is the initial state, which is known. This is the essence of the simple Markov chain model. In addition, it has been customary to assume that the chain is such that it is possible to go from any one state to every other state, but not necessarily in a single step.

Given the initial state of the system and the transition probabilities, it is obviously possible to compute the probability that the system will be in any state at any time in the future, for since

$$S_0 P = S_1$$
$$S_1 P = S_2$$

then

$$(S_0 P) = S_2$$

and so on. At the nth trial, $S_0 P^n = S_n$.

It is worth noting that if attention is focused on one element of the S matrix, call it s, the general form of the equation giving the time path of the element may be written as

$$s_t = \alpha^t s_0 + (1 - \alpha^t)\lambda,$$

where the parameters α and λ may be expressed in terms of the elements of the transition matrix.[4]

4. For proof of this, see Samuel Goldberg, *Introduction to Difference Equations*, John Wiley & Sons, Inc., New York, 1958, pp. 219–228.

Clearly, there is much more that can be said given this basic mathematical model. Maffei's article discusses some of these additional implications; Harary and Lipstein have also discussed this type of model.[5] Recently A. S. C. Ehrenberg has attempted to criticize this model[6] and W. F. Massey has presented empirical evidence that this model is not always an appropriate one.[7]

It is easy to take a particular specification of this model and raise questions about its validity. For example, Maffei specifies the model so that there are only two states. Maffei points out two assumptions: (1) changes in brand preference depend only on previous brand preference, and (2) P remains constant over time. These, of course, are assumptions inherent in the mathematical structure of the Markov chain model. There are actually two further assumptions Maffei makes in the use of this model that are at least as crucial as the two stated. First, he implicitly assumes constant purchase size over time; second, he lumps "everything else" into his second state, which confuses purchases of other brands with exit and entrance into the market.

The important point, however, is that this is not the only possible line of criticism of this model. Indeed, it is certainly not the most revealing. A model of consumer behavior has been presented here that purports to describe the behavior of consumers in the marketplace subjected to various promotional strategies of manufacturers and retailers. Nowhere is there any statement of

5. F. Harary and B. Lipstein, "The Dynamics of Brand Loyalty: A Markovian Approach," *Operations Research*, vol. 10, no. 1, January-February, 1962.

6. A. S. C. Ehrenberg, "An Appraisal of Markov Brand-Switching Models," *Journal of Marketing Research*, vol. 2, no. 4, November, 1965. Some of Ehrenberg's critical comments stem from neglect of the fact that the initial state must be given for a stochastic process to satisfy the definition of a Markov chain. See William Feller, *An Introduction to Probability Theory and Its Applications*, 2nd ed., vol. 1, John Wiley & Sons, Inc., New York, 1957, p. 340.

7. W. F. Massy, "Order and Homogeneity of Family Specific Brand-Switching Processes," *Journal of Marketing Research*, vol. 3, no. 1, February, 1966. It is worth noting that in his 1958 thesis, A. A. Kuehn also presented evidence that would not support this simple first-order Markov Chain theory. See A. A. Kuehn, *An Analysis of the Dynamics of Consumer Behavior and Its Implications for Marketing Management*, Carnegie Institute of Technology, Pittsburgh, Pennsylvania: Ph.D. thesis, 1958.

the behavioral assumptions that underlie this simple mathematical model. A fundamental question is, What is assumed about consumer behavior by the simple Markov Chain Model? The obvious next question is, Once these assumptions have been determined, are they sensible? If not, why not, and what can be done about it? It is to these questions that the ensuing discussion is directed.

An Introduction to the Concept of Adaptive Behavior

To achieve a clear understanding of how different assumptions lead to different theories of adaptive behavior, it is necessary to step backward and attempt to introduce the meaning that this book will attach to the term *adaptive behavior*. The definition used in this book is that adaptive behavior is equivalent to the capability to learn.[8]

The present purpose, of course, is to derive an empirically meaningful theory of consumer behavior. It deserves to be clearly stated that this section and the following ones are merely a review of existing knowledge, a review biased by the desire to show how the models to be discussed apply to consumer behavior, and not a proper introduction to mathematical learning theory. Indeed, the reader who is already well acquainted with mathematical learning theory may skip this section.[9]

A typical learning curve, in which the cumulative number of errors is plotted against the number of trials, will represent an obvious case for the fitting of a growth curve. For present purposes, interest must focus on deriving a simple underlying

8. E. R. Hilgard, *Theories of Learning*, Appleton-Century-Crofts, New York, 1956, provides a basic reference to psychological learning theory. Another book is William K. Estes et al., *Modern Learning Theory*, Appleton-Century-Crofts, New York, 1954.

9. The fundamental reference is R. R. Bush and F. Mosteller, *Stochastic Models for Learning*, John Wiley & Sons, Inc., New York, 1955. An elementary discussion of mathematical learning theory in general may be found in R. C. Atkinson, G. H. Bower, and E. J. Crothers, *An Introduction to Mathematical Learning Theory*, John Wiley & Sons, Inc., New York, 1965.

mechanism to explain the phenomenon. One way to start such a derivation is to abstract two fundamental notions from Hull's discussion of learning: that of an excitatory tendency that will, in a very crude sense, push toward giving the right answer, and that of an inhibitory tendency that has the opposite effect.[10] Further, it is postulated that there exists a mechanism that during the course of the learning experience produces a growing excitatory potential, a mechanism causing an inhibitory tendency, and finally a threshold concept. Given these preliminary statements, it is time to proceed to a specific statement.

Suppose p is the probability of a response during time k. This implies that learning is related to clock time. It is assumed that p is constant until response occurs. A response will change p. Responses, however, do not occur at a constant rate. This gives the theory a difficult twist. For this reason, probabilities are usually referred to trials, even though in some situations trials may correspond to time.

Given that $p(k)$ represents the probability of a response after the kth trial, and $p(k + 1)$ the probability of a response after the $(k + 1)^{th}$ trial, an operator Q may be defined that operates on $p(k)$ to produce $p(k + 1)$:

$$p(k + 1) = Qp(k).$$

This operator may be specified, given the postulates stated, as

$$Qp = p + a(1 - p) - bp = a + (1 - a - b)p, \qquad (2\text{-}2)$$

where $a(1 - p) =$ increment in excitatory potential
$bp =$ increment in inhibitory potential.[11]

10. Some readers may feel that an abstraction such as this does unjustified violence to Hull's theory. See C. L. Hull, *Principles of Behavior: An Introduction to Behavior Theory.* Appleton-Century-Crofts, New York, 1943. These models may be motivated in several ways other than by reference to Hull's work. See, for instance, Bush and Mosteller, *op. cit.*

11. For notational convenience, the $p(k)$ notation has been dropped in (2-2). The probabilities still refer to trials, however.

Consider, now, a pigeon rewarded whenever it pecks. What happens to this simple system over a series of pecks? The answer to this question can be derived by applying Q n times, starting from trial O.

$$Q^2p = Q(Qp) = a + (1 - a - b)p_1$$

and

$$p_1 = a + (1 - a - b)p_0$$

Hence,

$$Q^2p = a + (1 - a - b)a + (1 - a - b)^2p_0.$$

It is perfectly obvious,[12] therefore, that

$$Q^np = \frac{a}{a + b} - \left(\frac{a}{a + b} - p_0\right)(1 - a - b)^n.$$

12. That it is perfectly obvious may be seen as follows:

$$Q^3p = a[1 + (1 - a - b) + (1 - a - b)^2] + (1 - a - b)^3p_0$$

and

$$Q^np = a[1 + (1 - a - b) + (1 - a - b)^2 + \cdots + (1 - a - b)^{n-1}]$$
$$+ (1 - a - b)^np_0.$$

From the sum of a geometric progression,

$$Q^np = a\frac{(1 - a - b)^n - 1}{(1 - a - b) - 1} + (1 - a - b)^np_0$$

$$= \frac{a}{a + b} - \frac{a}{a + b}(1 - a - b)^n + (1 - a - b)^np_0$$

$$= \frac{a}{a + b} - \left(\frac{a}{a + b} - p_0\right)(1 - a - b)^n.$$

Note that these algebraic manipulations disclose clearly that the linear operator model will not usually produce a linear relationship between response probability and trial number.

The term $a + b$ is constrained to lie between zero and one. Therefore, as n approaches infinity, $(1 - a - b)^n$ approaches zero. It follows that the ultimate pecking rate is $a/(a + b)$.

Finally, suppose that after getting up to a certain pecking rate, the pigeon is no longer rewarded. Then only the extinction operator is operative:

$$Ep = p^* - bp^*$$

$$E^n p = (1 - b)^n p^*,$$

where p^* is the response probability at the point when reward ceases. Clearly as n approaches infinity, $E^n p$ approaches zero.

The reward operator itself may be written in different forms. Three of these are

$$Q_p = p + a(1 - p) - bp \qquad \text{Gain-loss form}$$

$$= a + (1 - a - b)p = a + \alpha p \qquad \text{Slope-intercept form}$$

$$= (1 - \alpha)\lambda + \alpha p \qquad \text{Fixed-point form}$$

The fixed-point form derives its name from the fact that if $p = \lambda$, $Q^i p = \lambda$. The expression λ is equal algebraically to $a/(a + b)$, which has been shown to be the long-run equilibrium probability of a correct response. Thus λ is interpretable as the long-run probability of response.

Certain restrictions are placed on the parameter values of the three forms. The parameter restrictions assuming non-oscillatory behavior are as follows:

$$0 \le a \le 1; \qquad 0 \le a + b \le 1 \qquad \text{Gain-loss form}$$

$$0 \le a \le 1; \qquad 0 \le \alpha \le 1 - a \qquad \text{Slope-intercept form}$$

$$0 \le \alpha \le 1; \qquad 0 \le \lambda \le 1 \qquad \text{Fixed-point form}$$

Finally, a simple numerical example may help make the

implications of the operator's operation clearer. For example, let $\lambda = 0.6$, $\alpha = 0.4$, and set the problem to be the computation of Qp for $p_0 = .5$ and $p_0 = .7$. The equation form is $Qp = \alpha p_0 + (1 - \alpha)\lambda$. Then

$$Qp = (.4)(.5) + (.6)(.6) = .56 \qquad \text{for } p_0 = .5$$

and

$$Qp = (.4)(.7) + (.6)(.6) = .64 \qquad \text{for } p_0 = .7.$$

It can be seen that application of Q brings p between p_0 and λ, given that $\alpha > 0$. Next, suppose that $\alpha = .3$ for the same values of p_0 as above. Then

$$Qp = (.3)(.5) + (.6)(.7) = .57 \qquad \text{for } p_0 = .5$$

and

$$Qp = (.3)(.7) + (.7)(.6) = .63 \qquad \text{for } p_0 = .7.$$

A higher value of $1 - \alpha$ implies a faster approach to the equilibrium value of the probability λ.

Sequences of Events: Constructing Useful Models from the Basic Bush–Mosteller Model

Consider now that there exist a set of alternatives A_j, identified with classes of responses, and a set of probability variables p_j corresponding to these alternatives. The simplest case would have only two alternatives, A_1 and A_2.

	A_1	A_2
Alternative		
Probability of response corresponding to alternative	p	$1 - p$

The probabilities alter according to operators applied, which correspond to occurrences of events.

Bush and Mosteller analyze operator sequences of several kinds. Among them are three that are basic for the present purposes:

1. Repetitive application of a single operator.
2. Experimenter control of the occurrence of events.
3. Subject control of the occurrence of events.

These three kinds of sequences will be briefly discussed. The goal of the discussion will be twofold: (1) to present an introduction to these models and (2), more important, to shed some light on the behavioral assumptions implicit in some of the recently advanced theories of adaptive consumer behavior.

Repetitive Application of a Single Operator

This case has been implicitly discussed in the previous section. It is reviewed here because (1) the algebraic manipulations involved are worth having a good feel for and (2) the implications of this model are worth further consideration.

Consider the case with two response classes A_1 and A_2 with probabilities p and $1 - p$ already diagrammed. The single event E_1 may be represented by an operator Q_1, so that

$$Q_1 p = \alpha_1 p + (1 - \alpha_1)\lambda_1.$$

If the probability of response A_1 before E_1 occurs is p, then $Q_1 p$ is the probability of that response after E_1 has occurred. Hence, if there is another occurrence of E_1, the operator Q_1 must be applied to the probability $Q_1 p$, so that

$$\begin{aligned} Q_1(Q_1 p) &= \alpha_1(Q_1 p) + (1 - \alpha_1)\lambda_1 \\ &= \alpha_1[\alpha_1 p + (1 - \alpha_1)\lambda_1] + (1 - \alpha_1)\lambda_1 \\ &= \alpha_1{}^2 p + (1 - \alpha_1{}^2)\lambda_1, \end{aligned}$$

and so on as, by assumption, E_1 occurs on each trial. After n trials,

$$Q_1{}^n p = \alpha_1{}^n p + (1 - \alpha_1{}^n)\lambda_1. \qquad (\mathbf{2\text{-}3})$$

$$\lim_{n \to \infty} Q_1{}^n p = \lambda_1 \qquad 0 < \alpha_1 < 1.$$

Next, the differential equation corresponding to this process will be derived and solved. Once the solution has been derived, its usefulness can be briefly discussed. Let $y = Q_1{}^n p$. Then $y + \Delta y = Q_1{}^{n+1} p$. Note that the independent variable is n. Thus,

$$Q_1{}^{n+1} p = \alpha_1 Q_1{}^n p + (1 - \alpha_1)\lambda_1.$$

Next, subtracting $Q_1{}^n p$ from both sides,

$$Q_1{}^{n+1} p - Q_1{}^n p = (1 - \alpha_1)(\lambda_1 - Q_1{}^n p)$$

or

$$\frac{(y + \Delta y) - y}{\Delta n} = \frac{\Delta y}{\Delta n} = (1 - \alpha_1)(\lambda_1 - y).$$

$$\frac{\Delta y}{\Delta n} \sim \frac{dy}{dn}.$$

Hence

$$\frac{dy}{dn} = (1 - \alpha_1)(\lambda_1 - y).$$

This has the solution

$$y = p_0 \exp\left[-(1 - \alpha_1)n\right] + \{1 - \exp\left[-(1 - \alpha_1)n\right]\}\lambda_1.$$

If $p_0 = 0$, the above equation is

$$y = \{1 - \exp[-(1 - \alpha_1)n]\}\lambda_1. \qquad (2\text{-}4)$$

This is the equation form used by Fourt and Woodlock in their study of the consumer response to new products.[13] They write (2-4) in the form

$$F(t) = (1 - e^{-\alpha t})\xi$$

and define $F(t)$ as the proportion of the whole population of households who have purchased a new product at least once within time t after its introduction to the market. At an individual level, assuming that the equative form for individuals and aggregates of individuals is the same, y would then be interpreted as the probability of an individual making a first purchase. Then E_1 could be identified as making a shopping tour through a store that stocked the new product and observing the new product.

One is, perhaps, tempted to say, "Aha! Now we understand the assumptions behind the Fourt and Woodlock theory." At this point, however, it is more useful to think of the statement as ending with a question mark, not a period, and to withhold such judgment temporarily until the case in which the experimenter controls the occurrence of events has been analyzed.

Experimenter Control of the Occurrence of Events

The situation that underlies this model may be best explained by imagining a consumer entering a simple T maze (Figure 2-1). Π_1 is the proportion of trials on which the consumer is rewarded

13. L. A. Fourt and J. W. Woodlock, "Early Prediction of Market Success for New Grocery Products," *Journal of Marketing*, vol. 26, no. 2, October, 1960. See also F. J. Anscombe, "Estimating a Mixed Exponential Response Law," *Journal of the American Statistical Association*, vol. 56, September, 1961, pp. 493–502. These articles also discuss purchase timing, an aspect of consumer behavior discussed in Chapter 4 of this book.

$1 - \pi_1$ π_1

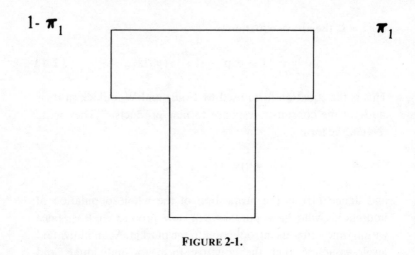

FIGURE 2-1.

for turning right, and is fixed by the experimenter. Let p represent the probability of a right turn. Finally, assume that a rewarded right turn or an unrewarded left turn constitutes a single event class, denoted E_1, with associated operator Q_1. Similarly an unrewarded right turn or a rewarded left turn constitutes an event class, denoted E_2, with associated operator Q_2. Given this structure, what is the probability of E_1? The expression $p\Pi_1$ is the probability of a rewarded right turn, $(1 - p)\Pi_1$ is the probability of an unrewarded left turn. The sum of these two is the probability of event E_1.

$$\text{Probability of } E_1 = p\Pi_1 + (1 - p)\Pi_1 = \Pi_1.$$

Similarly, the probability of event E_2 is readily seen to be $(1 - \Pi_1)$.

The next step is to demonstrate the effect of applying an operator Q_1 with fixed probability Π_1, and an operator Q_2 with fixed probability $\Pi_2 = 1 - \Pi_1$ on a group of consumers. That is, what is the average fraction of organisms that will make response A_1 after n applications of these operators?

After the first trial there would be two groups of consumers if the grouping is done on the basis of experience: those who underwent E_1 and those who underwent E_2. After the second trial, there would be four groups: E_1E_1, E_1E_2, E_2E_1, E_2E_2. Tracing this process onward, it may be seen that after n trials there would be 2^n groups at most if the simplifying presumption of equal initial probabilities for all people is made. Each of the 2^n groups is homogeneous in the sense that all animals in a group have the same probability of response A_1, but different groups have in general different response probabilities. It is convenient to think of the groups as being ordered after a particular number of applications of the operators. The notion that p_v is then the probability of response A_1 in the Vth group and P_v the proportion that the Vth group is of the total population may be meaningfully adopted. The average contribution of the Vth group to the total that would make response A_1 is just the product $P_v p_v$, and therefor the average fraction $\bar{p}_n$ for the entire population is simply the sum of such products over all the groups in the population. Thus,

$$\bar{p}_n = \sum_{v=1}^{2^n} p_v P_v$$

$$\bar{P}_0 = p \cdot 1 = p$$

$$\bar{P}_1 = \Pi_1 \cdot Q_1 p + \Pi_2 Q_2 p$$

$$\bar{p}_1 = \Pi_1(a_1 + \alpha_1 p) + \Pi_2(a_2 + \alpha_2 p)$$

$$\bar{p}_1 = \Pi_1 a_1 + \Pi_2 a_2 + (\Pi_1 \alpha_1 + \Pi_2 \alpha_2)p.$$

Let $\bar{p}_1 = \bar{a} + \bar{\alpha}p$, where $\bar{a}$ and $\bar{\alpha}$ are the averages of the a's and α's of the operators weighted by their frequencies of occurrence. Then it may be conjectured that

$$\bar{p}_n = \alpha^{-n}p + (1 - \alpha^{-n})\bar{\lambda}$$

where

$$\bar{\lambda} = \frac{\bar{\alpha}}{1 - \bar{\alpha}}.$$

To verify this conjecture, again introduce the notation that p_v is the probability of A_1 for the Vth group on the nth trial and that P_{vn} is the proportion: this group's size to the total group's size. Apply the operators on the $(n + 1)^{\text{st}}$ trial.

$$Q_1 p_{vn} = a_1 + \alpha_1 p_{vn}$$

$$Q_2 p_{vn} = a_2 + \alpha_2 p_{vn},$$

with new proportions $\Pi_1 P_{vn}$ and $\Pi_2 P_{vn}$, respectively.
Then

$$\bar{p}_{n+1} = \sum_{v=1}^{2^n} [\Pi_1 P_{vn}(a_1 + \alpha_1 p_{vn}) + \Pi_2 P_{vn}(a_2 + \alpha_2 p_{vn})]$$

$$= (\Pi_1 a_1 + \Pi_2 a_2) \sum_V P_{vn} + (\Pi_1 \alpha_1 + \Pi_2 \alpha_2) \sum_V P_{vn} p_{vn}.$$

But $\sum_V P_{vn} = 1$ and $\sum_V p_{vn} P_{vn} = \bar{p}_n$, so that

$$\bar{p}_{n+1} = \Pi_1 a_1 + \Pi_2 a_2 + (\Pi_1 \alpha_1 + \Pi_2 \alpha_2) \bar{p}_n$$

or

$$\bar{p}_{n+1} = \bar{a} + \bar{\alpha} \bar{p}_n.$$

This may be rewritten as

$$\bar{p}_n = \bar{\alpha}^n p + (1 - \bar{\alpha}^n) \bar{\lambda}. \tag{2-5}$$

Equation (2-5) is, in fact, the general form of the difference equation solution to a first-order Markov chain. Further, (2-5) has exactly the same form as (2-3). Only the interpretation placed upon the parameters differs. Equation (2-4) could also be derived from (2-5), just as it was from (2-3).

Finally, one special case of the general experimenter-controlled events model is worth brief discussion. Once again, reward of one response, when it occurs, is one event (E_1), and nonreward of that response, when it occurs, is the event E_2, so that there are only two events. Suppose now the sequence of events is set up according to a rule that if E_1 has just occurred, $p(E_1|E_1) =$ some constant fraction, and if E_2 occurs, $p(E_2|E_2) =$ some constant fraction. Assume also that the initial probability, $p_0(E_1)$, is known. Note that it is also required that the experiment be set up so as to create a one-to-one correspondence between events and responses. This set-up creates a simple Markov chain model of response. No more information is required, because

$$p_0(E_1) + p_0(E_2) = 1$$
$$p(E_1|E_1) + p(E_2|E_1) = 1$$
$$p(E_1|E_2) + p(E_2|E_2) = 1,$$

and hence only three probabilities are required, given the stated assumptions, because of the dependences listed. Thus,

$$p_1(E_1) = p_0(E_1)p(E_1|E_1) + p_0(E_2)p(E_1|E_2).$$

In general, on trial $n + 1$,

$$p_{n+1}(E_1) = p(E_1|E_2) + [p(E_1|E_1) - p(E_1|E_2)]p_n(E_1).$$

It is useful to interpret these p's as representing proportions of large numbers of things subjected to this experiment on a given trial. Following the notation of Bush and Mosteller,[14] let

$$p(E_1|E_2) = a$$

$$p(E_1|E_1) - p(E_1|E_2) = \alpha.$$

Then

$$p_{n+1}(E_1) = a + \alpha p_n(E_1),$$

which has the general solution

$$p_n(E_1) = \alpha^n p_0(E_1) + (1 - \alpha^n)p(E_1),$$

which is simply (2-5). This should hardly come as an overwhelming surprise because it has already been pointed out that this is a special case of the more general case of experimenter-controlled event occurrence. This discussion is intended to display clearly the correspondence between the aggregate equation form derivable from the experimenter-control situation and the Markov chain model of aggregate short-run behavior.

At this point it is useful to pause and review the substance of the argument. First, it has been shown that the Fourt–Woodlock model is indistinguishable from the Markov chain model in substance. This is a point that is not, perhaps, obvious in terms of the original discussion of these models. Second, it has been shown that at least two different underlying sets of behavioral assumptions, the one-event repetitive-sequence model and the experimenter-controlled model, lead to the same aggregate response equation. (Such a result is well known to psychologists.) Third, and this is the important point, both these models are nonsense as acceptable models of consumer behavior in the marketplace. The traditional economic theory of consumer behavior places great importance on the concept of the consumer's

14. Bush and Mosteller, op. cit., p. 75.

maximizing a utility function derivable from consumer preferences that are controlled by the consumer. This is without doubt one of the reasons the traditional theory has such great strength: Its assumptions about how preferences are formed are really quite sensible. The Markov chain model, just the opposite, assumes the consumer *reacts* to rewards given him in the marketplace, without having any voice in whether product use is satisfying or not.

To sum up, the fundamental criticism of the simple Markov chain model of consumer behavior must be that the assumptions upon which it rests are nonsense. It can be hardly surprising that the empirical evidence suggests that a Markov chain is not a sensible theory of consumer behavior.

The preceding statement is not intended as destructive criticism. Rather, it is intended to focus attention on the really important question: What is a sensible model, if a Markov chain with "brands bought" as states is not? The next section is intended to propose one possible answer to this question.

Subject Control of the Occurrence of Events

The obvious answer to the critique is to develop a model of adaptive behavior in which response occurrence is equated with an event. In this case, reward is thought of as being contingent upon the occurrence of a particular response. In terms of the T maze used as an example in the case of experimenter control, this condition could be met by having reward always found for a right turn. The event includes the outcome and the response, but the outcome of a trial is completely determined by the response that the organism, i.e., consumer, makes. "Hence, we can say that E_1 occurs whenever A_1 occurs and that E_2 occurs whenever A_2 occurs. For this reason we refer to this case as the case of subject-controlled events."[15]

15. *Ibid.*, p. 76. It is useful to recall that Chapter 1 of this book contained a specific application of this model to the problem of understanding consumer behavior in a supermarket.

As before, it is first interesting to inquire what the probability is that event E_1 will occur after n trials. Let $\bar{p}_0 = p$. Then, as before,

$$\begin{aligned}
\bar{p}_1 &= pQ_1p + (1 - p)Q_2p \\
&= p(a_1 + \alpha_1 p) + (1 - p)(a_2 + \alpha_2 p) \\
&= a_1 p + \alpha_1 p^2 + a_2 + \alpha_2 p - a_2 p - \alpha_2 p^2 \\
&= a_2 + (a_1 - a_2 + \alpha_2)p + (\alpha_1 - \alpha_2)p^2.
\end{aligned}$$

It may be readily seen that the average value of the probability on higher trails will be a function of higher and higher powers of p, as high as the number of times the operators have been applied plus one. The expression for p_n is no longer linear in p_{n-1}, and so on.

The next problem is to attempt to derive the average fraction of consumers that will make response A_1 after n applications of the operators.

As before, let P_{vn} be the probability of occurrence of the response probability p_{vn} on trial n. (Think of a large population of identical consumers undergoing the same learning process.) Then P_{vn} is the proportion of this population that has the probability value p_{vn} on trial n.

By definition, the mth moment V_m is

$$V_m = \sum_v p_v{}^m P_v. \tag{2-6}$$

Now recall that the case being considered is that of two subject-controlled events. Let the probability of application of Q_1 be identical with the probability value at the time. If the operators are applied once more, the new proportions (probabilities of response) are $p_{vn}P_{vn}$ with respect to Q_1 and $(1 - p_{vn})P_{vn}$ with respect to Q_2.

The mth moment on trial $n + 1$ can be evaluated by summing the product of the mth power of the new probability values with the proportions

$$V_{m,n+1} = \sum_{V=1}^{2^n} (Q_1 p_{vn})^m p_{vn} P_{vn} + \sum_{V=1}^{2^n} (Q_2 p_{vn})^m (1 - p_{vn}) P_{vn}$$

$$= \sum_V (a_1 + \alpha_1 p_{vn})^m p_{vn} P_{vn} + \sum_V (a_2 + \alpha_2 P_{vn})^m (1 - p_{vn}) P_{vn}.$$

Since

$$(x - y)^m = \sum_{u=0}^{m} (-1)^u \binom{m}{u} x^{m-u} y^u,$$

$$V_{m,n+1} = \sum_v \sum_{u=0}^{m} \binom{m}{u} a_1^{m-u} \alpha_1^u p^{u+1} P_{vn}$$

$$- \sum_v \sum_{u=0}^{m} \binom{m}{u} a_2^{m-u} \alpha_2^u p_{vn}^{u+1} P_{vn}$$

$$+ \sum \sum_{u=0}^{m} \binom{m}{u} a_2^{m-u} \alpha_2^u p_{vn}^u P_{vn}.$$

Using (2-6), sum on V in each of the three sums above

$$V_{m,n+1} = \sum_{u=0}^{m} \binom{m}{u} a_2^{m-u} \alpha_1^u V_{u+1,n}$$

$$- \sum_{u=0}^{m} \binom{m}{u} a_2^{m-u} \alpha_2^u V_{u+1,n} + \sum_{u=0}^{m} \binom{m}{u} a_2^{m+u} \alpha_2^{m+u} V_{u,n}.$$

$$(2\text{-}7)$$

This equation can be written in a more convenient form by collecting together the terms $V_{1,n}$, $V_{2,n}$, and so forth, on the right side of (2-7). To do this it is necessary to determine a set of coefficients $C_{m,u}$, which will allow the equation to be rewritten as

$$V_{m,n+1} = \sum_{u=0}^{m} C_{m,u} V_{u,n}.$$

To do this, first change the dummy index from u to v in the first two sums on the right of (2-7), and rewrite it.

$$V_{m,n+1} = \sum_{v=0}^{m} \binom{m}{v} (a_1^{m-v}\alpha_1^{v} - a_2^{m-v}\alpha_2^{m-v})V_{v+1,n}$$

$$+ \sum_{u=0}^{m} \binom{m}{u} a_2^{m-u}\alpha_2^{u} V_{u,n}.$$

Let $v = u - 1$; then

$$V_{m,n+1} = \sum_{u=1}^{m+1} \binom{m}{u-1} a_1^{m-u+1}\alpha_1^{u-1} - a_2^{m-u+1}\alpha_2^{u-1}V_{u,n}$$

$$+ \sum_{u=0}^{m} \binom{m}{u} a_2^{m-u}\alpha_2^{u}V_{u,n}.$$

Then separate out the terms for $u = 0$ in the last sum and for $u - m + 1$ in the first sum and combine the other terms.

$$V_{m,n+1} = a_2^{m}V_{o,n} + \sum_{u=1}^{m} \left[\binom{m}{u-1}(a_1^{m-u+1}\alpha_1^{u-1} - a_2^{m-u+1}\alpha_2^{u-1}) \right.$$

$$\left. + \binom{m}{u} a_2^{m-u}\alpha_2^{u} \right] V_{u,n} + (\alpha_1^{m} - \alpha_2^{m})V_{m+1,n}.$$

Therefore,

$$C_{m,u} = \begin{cases} \alpha_2^{m} & u = 0 \\ \binom{m}{u-1} a_1^{m-u+1}\alpha_1^{u-1} - a_2^{m-u+1}\alpha_2^{u-1} \\ \quad + \binom{m}{u} a_2^{m-u}\alpha_2^{u} & u = 1,2,\ldots,m \\ = \alpha_1^{m} - \alpha_2^{m}. & u = m+1 \end{cases}$$

The mean on trial $n + 1$ is, therefore,

$$V_{1,n+1} = a_2 + (a_1 - a_2 + \alpha_2)V_{1,n} + (\alpha_1 - \alpha_2)V_{2,n}, \quad \textbf{(2-8)}$$

and the second raw moment is

$$V_{2,n+1} = a_2^2 + (a_1^2 - a_2^2 + 2\alpha_1\alpha_2)V_{1,n}$$
$$+ [2(a_1\alpha_1 - a_2\alpha_2) + \alpha_2^2]V_{2,n} + (\alpha_1^2 - \alpha_2^2)V_{3,n} \quad \textbf{(2-9)}$$

and so on for higher moments. The recurrence formula for the mean is a function of higher moments than the mean.[16]

It is useful to pause and look carefully at the dilemma implied by (2-8) and (2-9). These equations imply not only that the recurrence formula for the mean is a function of higher moments but also that it is a function of the observed moments on all previous trials ($V_{2,n}$ is a function of $V_{1,n-1}$, $V_{2,n-1}$, and $V_{3,n-1}$, and so on).

Thus a simple first-order process in the case of the individual becomes a process of very high order when the behavior of individuals is aggregated.

The basic reason for this is that on any given response occasion other than the first, consumers will differ from one another in terms of their response probabilities. This is an unequivocal prediction of the theory developed in this section. Thus, to argue that response heterogeneity, i.e., consumers' having different probabilities of choosing a brand, shows that learning-theory models of consumer behavior are incorrect is totally wrong.[17] In fact, the theory predicts response heterogeneity.

16. The basic reference for the above derivation is Bush and Mosteller, *op. cit.*, pp. 94–96.

17. Further discussion of this issue may be found in D. G. Morrison, *Stochastic Models for Time Series with Applications in Marketing*, Technical Report no. 8, Program in Operations Research, Stanford University, Stanford, California, August 30, 1965.

The problem to be dealt with has now altered. It has been shown that what would appear to be a reasonable model of consumer behavior encounters analytic difficulties, whereas what seems to be an unreasonable model of consumer behavior behaves very nicely analytically. This is undoubtedly one of the reasons for the popularity of the simple Markov chain model. The question to be answered is, How can these difficulties be resolved? This is the central question answered in the next chapter.

Chapter 3

Extension of the Adaptive Model of Consumer Behavior

The previous chapters have argued that any reasonable theory of consumer behavior in market situations must grant to the consumer the right of self-determination of tastes. Further, it has been shown that the simplest adaptive model having this characteristic presents an aggregation problem when one tries to examine its implications for groups of consumers. This chapter considers in detail two solutions that have been proposed for this aggregation problem. It also discusses some extensions of the basic model, within the framework of these solutions, that show how marketing policies of firms affect consumer choice. Two solutions have arisen from considering different causal factors that may alter consumer preferences. The first is based on the effect that advertising, promotions, distribution policy, and product policy may have on altering consumer preferences, given a group of existing brands. The second proposed solution results from an attempt to apply the basic theoretical concepts to the problem of understanding consumer response to new-product introduction.

The Aggregate Consumer

The first approach presumes an aggregate consumer and was explicated by A. A. Kuehn in the context of demonstrating how an understanding of consumer behavior may be used by firms to set advertising budgets.[1]

The fundamental concept is that considered in the previous chapter: Compute the mathematical expectation of the probability value on trial 1, using this mean probability value for the probability of applying the success operator on trial 1 to obtain an average probability value on trial 2, and so on.[2] It has already been shown in Chapter 2 that this does not yield tractable results for subject-controlled events. If, however, certain additional assumptions are made, the intractability can be assumed away. Kuehn proposes the following subject-controlled linear operator model to describe consumer behavior:

1. Assume a gain operator that is applied when brand i is the brand purchased on the last buying occasion. If the characteristics of the product are such as to give positive reward in use, this operator will typically increase the probability that brand i will be purchased in the future. The gain operator has the form

$$P_{i,t} = P_{i,t-1} + g(U_i - P_{i,t-1}). \qquad (3\text{-}1)$$

2. Also assume a loss operator that is applied when some brand other than i was purchased on the last buying

1. A. A. Kuehn, "A Model for Budgeting Advertising," in F. M. Bass et al., eds., *Mathematical Models and Methods in Marketing*, Richard D. Irwin, Inc., Homewood, Illinois, 1961, pp. 315–348.

2. R. R. Bush and F. Mosteller, *Stochastic Models for Learning*, John Wiley & Sons, Inc., New York, 1955, p. 138.

occasion. Typically, this operator reduces the probability of brand i's being purchased in the future.

However, if the alternative brand bought proves unsatisfactory, this need not be the case. The operator has the form

$$P_{i,t} = P_{i,t-1} - \ell(P_{i,t-1} - L_i), \qquad (3\text{-}2)$$

$$0 \leq L_i \leq P_{i,t-1} \leq U_i \leq 1; \qquad 0 \leq g, \ell \leq 1$$

where $P_{i,t}$ = probability of the consumer's purchasing brand i on the tth purchase occasion

g = gain parameter, the fraction of maximum possible gain in purchase probability $(U - P_{i,t-1})$ that is realized when the brand is purchased

ℓ = loss parameter, analogous to g

U_i = upper limit of probability of purchasing brand i

L_i = lower limit of probability of purchasing brand i.

It should be noted that this is merely writing the operators in slope-intercept form, for

$$P_{i,t} = P_{i,t-1} + g(U_i - P_{i,t-1})$$
$$= gU_i + (1 - g)P_{i,t-1},$$

and therefore, in terms of the notation of Chapter 2,

$$a_{1i} = gU_i \qquad \text{and} \qquad \alpha_{1i} = 1 - g.$$

Similarly,

$$a_{2i} = \ell L_i \qquad \text{and} \qquad \alpha_{2i} = 1 - \ell.$$

A second comment to help clarify the above discussion is in order. Kuehn's description of the gain operator as increasing the probability of brand i's being purchased in the future is true only if $P_{i,t-1} < U_i$. If $P_{i,t-1} = U_i$, $P_{i,t} = U_i$, if the product is bought again. If $P_{i,t-1} > U_i$, application of the gain operator will *reduce* the probability of brand i's being purchased in the future.

Similarly, the loss operator will cause a decrease in the probability of brand i being purchased only as long as $P_{i,t-1} > L_i$. If $P_{i,t-1} < L_i$, application of the loss operator will *increase* the probability of brand i being purchased in the future, and if $P_{i,t-1} = L_i$, application of the loss operator leaves unchanged the probability of brand i's being purchased in the future.[3]

The gain and loss operators can be combined, each weighted by its probability of being operative, to yield the expected value purchase-probability relationship

$$P_{i,t} = P_{i,t-1}[P_{i,t-1} + g(U_i - P_{i,t-1})]$$
$$+ (1 - P_{i,t-1})[P_{i,t-1} - \ell(P_{i,t-1} - L_i)].$$

Simplifying,

$$P_{i,t} = (\ell - g)P_{i,t-1}^2 + (1 + gU_i - \ell - \ell L_i)P_{i,t-1} + \ell L_i. \quad (3\text{-}3)$$

The next step is to assume that g_i and ℓ_i are constant for all brands. This implies that $g = \ell$, and therefore (3-3) reduces to

$$P_{i,t} = P_{i,t-1}[1 - g(1 - U_i + L_i)] + gL_i. \quad (3\text{-}4)$$

Finally, it is argued that $P_{i,t}$ is interpretable as the proportional of all consumers who will purchase, not the probability of a single consumer's purchasing, by presuming the parameters in (3-4) to be defined for all consumers, not for a single consumer. In other words, the aggregation problem is solved by asserting that the

---

3. Misunderstanding of this aspect of the operator's operations has occasioned some unnecessary criticism of this model. See, for example, R. J. Lawrence, "Models of Consumer Purchasing Behavior," *Applied Statistics*, vol. 15, no. 3, November, 1966, pp. 216–233.

aggregate equation form can be approximated by the individual equation form.

There is more to the argument than this. Recalling the basic solution to the aggregation problem given in Chapter 2,

$$V_{1,n+1} = A_2 + (a_1 - a_2 + \alpha_2)V_{1,n} + (\alpha_1 - \alpha_2)V_{2,n}, \quad (2\text{-}8)$$

it may be clearly seen that if the two learning rates were equal, the aggregate equation would also be first-order. Once g has been set equal to ℓ, however, the two learning rates have been set equal. Thus (3-4) follows directly from (2-8) once the assumption of equal learning rates has been made.

Equation (3-4) may be rewritten in fixed-point form as

$$P_{i,t} = rP_{i,t-1} + (1 - r)a_i. \quad (3\text{-}5)$$

In (3-5), r is analogous to α in Chapter 2, and a_i to λ_i. Different symbols are used here because (3-5) refers to aggregate, not individual, behavior. Kuehn interprets r as a retention factor, i.e., as a measure of brand loyalty, and a_i as a merchandising attraction fraction.[4]

4. The relationship between the parameters in (3-4) and (3-5) is the following:

$$r = 1 - g(1 - U_i + L_i)$$
$$a_i = gL_i \quad (1\text{-}4)$$

or

$$[1 - (1 - g + gU_i - gL_i)]a_i = gL_i.$$

Simplifying,

$$(g - gU_i + gL_i)a_i = gL_i.$$

Cancelling the g's, and rearranging,

$$a_i = \frac{L_i}{1 - U_i + L_i}.$$

Equation (3-5) refers to the aggregate probability of brand i's being bought. Suppose both sides of (3-5) are multiplied by the number of families in the market (F) and by the average purchase size per family (PS), then an equation relating sales of brand i to time may be derived.

$$S_{i,t} = (F)(PS)P_{i,t} = S_{i,t-1}(r) + (1 - r)(F)(PS)a_i$$

$(F)(PS) = $ unit sales of all brands, time$_{t-1} = I_{t-1}$. The final result is

$$S_{i,t} = S_{i,t-1}(r) + I_{t-1}(1 - r)Z_{i,T} \qquad (3\text{-}6)$$

where, of course, $Z_{i,T} = a_i$.

Equation (3-6) is the first fundamental result. It expresses the time path of sales of a brand in a market, given the assumption that individual consumers behave according to the underlying subject-controlled learning model.

It should be noted before proceeding further that the subject-controlled learning model is equivalent to a first-order Markov chain model with the states of the system being the possible values

---

Finally, if there is a closed-market system, i.e.,

$$g = \ell \qquad \text{and} \qquad U_i = 1 - \sum_{j \neq i} L_j,$$

then

$$a_i = \frac{L_i}{1 - \left(1 - \sum_{j \neq i} L_j\right) + L_i} = \frac{L_i}{\Sigma L_i}$$

$$r = 1 - g\left[1 - \left(1 - \sum_{j \neq i} L_j\right) + L_i\right] = 1 - g[\Sigma L_i]$$

$$1 - r = 1 - (1 - g\Sigma L_i) = g\Sigma L_i.$$

of the response probability. This is not a Markov chain model that has "brands available" as states. As has been shown in Chapter 2, the difference is real and meaningful.[5]

The final step in the Kuehn model is to present a theoretical statement of what determines a_i or $Z_{i,T}$. In order to comprehend fully the meaning of this final step, it is necessary to introduce a brief digression on individual choice behavior.

Individual Choice Behavior

The parameter a_i, or $Z_{i,T}$ has been shown to represent the long-run probability of a consumer's buying the brand under consideration. That is, it reflects individual choice behavior in the situation where the consumer has been "pretrained" so that he is able to discriminate between alternatives. Now we want to consider an abstract model of choice behavior in such situations. Note that in the beginning, when the traditional theory of consumer behavior was discussed, a deterministic theory of choice behavior in such situations was used. The theory to be discussed here is that of R. D. Luce.[6] This theory is one of probabilistic, i.e., stochastic, choice.[7]

The basic ingredients for a choice situation or experiment of this type are a set of k alternatives (e.g., different brands of canned peas on a store shelf) and a consumer who chooses from the set. In a laboratory situation, the subject is presented repeatedly with various subsets of k alternatives and asked to make a choice. There would be $\binom{k}{2}$ subsets of two stimuli, $\binom{k}{3}$

5. Peter A. Longton and B. T. Warner, "A Mathematical Model for Marketing," *Metra*, vol. 1, no. 3, September, 1962, express the opposite viewpoint.

6. R. D. Luce, *Individual Choice Behavior*, John Wiley & Sons, Inc., New York, 1959. An introductory exposition of this theory is Chapter 4 in R. C. Atkinson, G. H. Bower, and E. J. Crothers, *An Introduction to Mathematical Learning Theory*, John Wiley & Sons, Inc., New York, 1965.

7. A detailed discussion of a stochastic choice theory in a context of the experimenter-controlled (i.e., "simple" Markov chain) situations may be found in Patrick Suppes, "Behavioristic Foundations of Utility," *Econometrica*, vol. 29, no. 2, April, 1961.

subsets of three stimuli, and so on. The experimenter would prepare a particular presentation schedule that would specify which subset would be presented on each trial. Usually this schedule would be determined by random selection, without replacement, from the subsets of interests. The datum recorded is the alternative selected by the subject when confronted with each presentation set. In a shopping situation, a consumer is presented repeatedly, over time and in different stores, with various subsets of alternatives and asked to make a choice. The essential difference is that the presentation schedule faced by a consumer is dependent upon store policies, manufacturer policies, and so on. That is, to use the terminology of Cartwright and Zander, the difference is the traditional difference between a laboratory experiment and a field experiment.[8]

As has been pointed out, it is usually assumed that the subjects' choices over successive presentations are stochastically independent. This implies that the subjects' choices are not influenced by the trial sequence in which the various presentation sets occur.

A Formal Statement of the Choice Axiom

Let x, y, z, t, u = alternatives

T = the total set of all alternatives

R = a subset of T

$Pr(x; R)$ = the probability that x is chosen when the choice is restricted to the set R ($x \in R$ by assumption)

$Pr(x; y)$ = the probability that x is chosen when only x and y are presented as possible choices.

Then, Luce's axiom is

$$Pr(x; T) = Pr(R; T)Pr(x; R). \qquad (3\text{-}7)$$

8. D. Cartwright and A. Zander, *Group Dynamics*, 2d. ed., Harper & Row, Publishers, New York, 1960, pp. 48–56.

The product of the probability that some element of R is chosen when T is presented and the probability of choosing x from the set R is the probability of choosing alternative x from the entire set T. It can be seen that (3-7) can be tested directly by appropriate experiments. Equation (3-7) also implies and is implied by ratio-scale measurement of utility. To see this, begin by choosing any arbitrary element a of T. Then define the strength of x, denoted by $v(x)$, as

$$v(x) = \frac{Pr(x, a)}{Pr(a, x)} = \frac{Pr(x; T)}{Pr(a; T)}.$$

From this definition it follows that

$$\frac{v(x)}{v(y)} = \frac{Pr(x; T)}{Pr(a; T)} \cdot \frac{Pr(a; T)}{Pr(y; T)} = \frac{Pr(x; T)}{Pr(y; T)} = \frac{Pr(x, y)}{Pr(y, x)}$$

where the last equality follows from (3-7). This result may be used to provide an alternative expression to (3-7) for $Pr(x; T)$.

$$Pr(x; T) = \frac{1}{\displaystyle\sum_y \frac{Pr(y, x)}{Pr(x, y)}} \frac{1}{\displaystyle\sum_y \frac{v(y)}{v(x)}} = \frac{v(x)}{\displaystyle\sum_y v(y)}.$$

To summarize,

$$Pr(x; T) = \frac{v(x)}{\displaystyle\sum_y v(y)}. \tag{3-8}$$

Equation (3-8) has the following implication: If a set of choice probabilities conforms to the implications of Luce's axiom, then numbers, $v(x)$, can be assigned to the alternatives in such a manner that these numbers reflect the choice probabilities and are unique except for multiplication by a positive constant. That is, the v's form what is called a *ratio scale* of measurement.[9] Equation (3-8) is the form in which Luce's choice axiom has been applied in marketing problems. The first application of it was by A. A. Kuehn, who proposed a specific form of (3-8) applicable to consumer choice in the marketplace.[10] A second important application of Luce's choice axiom is that of David L. Huff, who shows that this axiom is applicable to the problem of understanding, explaining, and predicting the spatial behavior of consumers.[11] Huff's basic form of $v(x)$ is

$$v(j) = \frac{S_j}{T_{ij}^{\lambda}}$$

where λ = a sensitivity of difference discrimination parameter[12]

S_j = the size of retail location j

T_{ij} = the distance separating the consumer i and the retail location j

n = number of retail locations considered.

Thus, the probability that a consumer living at location i will choose to shop at the location j is simply

$$P_{ij} = \frac{S_j/T_{ij}^{\lambda}}{\sum_{j=1}^{n} S_j/T_{ij}^{\lambda}}.$$

The empirical evidence available supports the above equation as a reasonable explanation of consumer spatial behavior. However, very little work has been done on the dynamics of consumer spatial behavior, although clearly it might be sus-

9. Atkinson, Bower, and Crothers, *op. cit.*, Ch. 4.

10. A. A. Kuehn, "An Analysis of the Dynamics of Consumer Behavior and Its Implications for Marketing Management," Carnegie Institute of Technology, Pittsburgh, Pennsylvania: Ph.D. thesis, 1958.

11. David L. Huff, *Determination of Intraurban Retail Trade Areas*, University of California, Los Angeles, Real Estate Research Program, 1962.

12. Luce, *op. cit.*, esp. pp. 42–45.

pected that the theory already presented should be of some explanatory value in this area.[13]

The Determination of $Z_{i,T}$

Given the previous digression, it is now possible to proceed with the discussion of the Kuehn model. Actually, all that is required is to present the specification of $v(x)$ that Kuehn uses. This should be really a very simple matter; and so it is in fact, despite the complex appearance of the result. First, it is necessary to make note of what factors might affect the utility in use of a consumer product. Such a list of factors, Kuehn argues, includes the product's characteristics in use, its price, its distribution and display space in stores, and possibly its advertising. Further, a product must have both price and availability for it to be a meaningful alternative. The specification of $v(x)$ may be written down after the following symbols have been defined:

P'_i = relative appeal to consumers of the product character- istics of brand i

p_i = price of brand i

ε_P = a measure of consumer responsiveness to price

$P_i = KP'_i(p_i^{-\varepsilon_P}/\sum_i p_i^{-\varepsilon_P})$ = relative appeal to consumers of price and product characteristics of brand i

D_i = relative appeal to consumers of distribution, display, and so on, of brand i

ε_D = a measure of consumer responsiveness to distribution

A_i = relative appeal to consumers of advertising of brand i

ε_A = a measure of consumer responsiveness to advertising.

13. Two references that do address the dynamics of consumer behavior are Robert F. Kelly, "The Diffusion Model as a Predictor of Ultimate Patronage Levels in New Retail Outlets," in Raymond M. Haas, ed., *Science, Technology, and Marketing*, American Marketing Association, 230 N. Michigan Avenue, Chicago, Illinois, January, 1967; and Fred C. Allvine, *The Patronage Decision-Making Process*, Indiana University, Bloomington, Indiana: unpublished DBA dissertation, 1966.

Thus,

$$v(i) = P_i D_i^{\varepsilon_D} A_i^{\varepsilon_A}. \qquad (3\text{-}9)$$

If $\varepsilon_D = \varepsilon_A = 1$, then clearly $Z_{i,T}$ is the following:[14]

$$Z_{i,T} = \frac{(PDA)_i}{\sum\limits_i (PDA)_i} \qquad (3\text{-}10)$$

where, it must be recalled, it is assumed that $Z_{i,T}$ holds for the aggregate of consumers in the market.

There are two further elaborations to make. First, (3-10) assumes that all consumers are exposed to and influenced by advertising. If some fraction b_{PD} of consumers is not exposed to or influenced by advertising, then (3-10) may be written

$$Z_{i,T} = b_{PD}(PD)_i + b_{PDA}\frac{(PDA)_i}{\sum\limits_i (PDA)_i} \qquad (3\text{-}11)$$

where $b_{PDA} = 1 - b_{PD}$ and $\sum\limits_i (PD)_i = 1$ by normalization convention. Equation (3-11) is the basic equation for $Z_{i,T}$ presented by Kuehn in "A Model for Budgeting Advertising." Second, entry into the market and exit from it may be readily allowed for in this model. Although this is a very simple matter and is the last extension of the model to be made, it is of great practical importance. Fundamental demographic factors, such as the life-cycle stage of families, should never be overlooked in attempting to understand the determinants of a product's sales.[15]

14. The assumption that $\varepsilon_D = \varepsilon_A = 1$ was made in Kuehn "A Model for Budgeting Advertising," apparently to make exposition easier, but is relaxed in later statements of the model. Cf. for instance, A. A. Kuehn and D. L. Weiss, "Marketing Analysis Training Exercise," *Behavioral Science*, vol. 10, no. 1, January, 1965.
15. See, for instance, Ralph L. Day, *Marketing Models*, International Textbook Co., Scranton, Pennsylvania, 1964, part IID.

Let e = probability of survival of past customers

g = entry of potential customers to the market for the product as a fraction of the size of the market in the previous time period.

Then (3-6), (3-11), and exist and entry may be combined to yield the final result[16]

$$S_{i,t} = r_i e S_{i,t-1} + I_{t-1}[g + (1 - \bar{r}_t)e]b_{P\dot{D}}(PD)_i$$

$$+ I_{t-1}[g + (1 - \bar{r}_t)e]b_{PDA} \frac{(PDA)_i}{\Sigma(PAA)_i}. \qquad (3\text{-}12)$$

The meaning of (3-12) is quite simple. Sales volume for a brand i during time period t is composed of three elements: (1) surviving loyal customers of the previous period, (2) newcomers and surviving potential brand shifters attracted to or retained by the brand as a result of the brand's product characteristics, price, and retail availability, and (3) newcomers and surviving potential brand shifters attracted to the brand as a result of the brand's product characteristics, price, retail availability, and advertising.[17] This completes the exposition of the Kuehn approach to solving the aggregation problem. Discussion of certain technical details, such as measuring product characteristic appeal, is deferred until Chapter 5, and discussion of empirical estimation procedures and results is contained in Chapter 4.

A Second Solution

We now turn to a second proposed solution to the aggregation problem. This solution is motivated by a desire to apply

16. $\bar{r}_t$ is the weighted average of decay rate for the whole industry; it is not necessarily constant and equal to r for all brands unless the conditions described for what Kuehn calls a *closed-market system* are met.

17. Kuehn, "A Model for Budgeting Advertising," pp. 326–327.

the basic concept to understanding response to new-product introduction, and was proposed by the present author.[18]

This second approach presumes two operators. (1) A purchase operator Q_1 that modifies the probability of the new product being purchased in the future. This operator is applied when the new product was purchased on the last buying occasion.

$$Q_1 p_t = p_{t+1} = \alpha p_t + (1 - \alpha_1)\lambda_1$$

(2) A nonpurchase operator Q_2 that does not modify the probability of the new product being purchased in the future. This operator is applied whenever the new product was not purchased on the last buying occasion.

$$Q_2 p_t = p_{t+1} = p_t$$

The nonpurchase operator requires some justification. The argument is as follows: One of the attributes of newness is that consumers are not aware of close technical substitutes or complements for the new product. Therefore, the decision to use or not to use the product is made on the basis of the new product alone. If the new product has close technical substitutes or complements of which the consuming public is aware, then the nonpurchase operator would have to have the form of (3-2). Finally, the proposed specification must, therefore, only apply to the introductory period. One rule of thumb used by some people concerned with actual new-product introduction is that this introductory period has a maximum length of one year for consumer nondurables.

Given this specification, a solution to the aggregation problem is implied. The solution proceeds as follows: First recall that for the particular specification of the subject-controlled

18. George H. Haines, Jr., "A Theory of Market Behavior After Innovation," *Management Science*, vol. 10, no. 4, July, 1964.

linear operator model already presented,

$$\alpha_2 = 1, \qquad a_1 = \lambda_1(1 - \alpha_1), \qquad \alpha_1 = \alpha_1, \qquad a_2 = 0.$$

Therefore,

$$V_{1,n+1} = a_2 + (a_1 - a_2 + \alpha_2)V_{1,n} + (\alpha_1 - \alpha_2)V_{2,n} \quad (\textbf{2-8})$$

reduces to

$$V_{1,n+1} = [1 + \lambda_1(1 - \alpha_1)]V_{1,n} - (1 - \alpha_1)V_{2,n}. \quad (\textbf{3-13})$$

The fundamental aggregation difficulty of Chapter 2—that the recurrence formula for the mean is a function of higher moments than the mean—remains.

One way to obtain an approximation to (3-13) is to apply the operators directly to the means, computing a weighted average of the operations $Q_1 V_{1,n}$ and $Q_2 V_{1,n}$, with weights $V_{1,n}$ and $1 - V_{1,n}$, respectively. That is,

$$\bar{Q}V_{1,n} = V_{1,n}Q_1 V_{1,n} + (1 - V_{1,n})Q_2 V_{1,n}.$$

Using the slope-intercept form of the operators, Bush and Mosteller obtain[19]

$$\bar{Q}V_{1,n} = V_{1,n}(a_1 + \alpha_1 V_{1,n}) + (1 - V_{1,n})(a_2 + \alpha_2 V_{1,n})$$

$$= a_2 + (a_1 - a_2 + \alpha_2)V_{1,n} + (\alpha_1 - \alpha_2)V_{1,n}{}^2. \quad (\textbf{3-14})$$

Assume that $V_{1,n+1} = \bar{Q}V_{1,n}$. Then

$$\frac{dV_{1,n}}{dn} \simeq \bar{Q}V_{1,n} - V_{1,n}$$

$$= a_2 + (a_1 - a_2 + \alpha_2 - 1)V_{1,n} + (\alpha_1 - \alpha_2)V_{1,n}{}^2. \quad (\textbf{3-15})$$

19. Bush and Mosteller, *op. cit.*, p. 138.

For the special case under consideration, (3-15) reduces to

$$\frac{dV_{1,n}}{dn} \simeq \lambda_1(1 - \alpha_1)V_{1,n} - (1 - \alpha_1)V_{1,n}{}^2. \qquad (3\text{-}16)$$

It should be noted that in defining the new operator $\bar{Q}$, it is no longer necessary that all individual parameters be equal. Of course, if they are all equal, the derivation is unaffected. However, if the averages are actually operated upon by average parameters, the result in (3-16) still follows.[20] Equation (3-16) is, of course, simply the differential equation form of the classical logistic curve.[21] This equation may be explicitly solved by separation of variables.[22]

Let Y represent $V_{1,n}$ and, dropping the approximately equal sign,

$$\frac{dY}{(1 - \alpha_1)\lambda Y - (1 - \alpha_1)Y^2} = dn.$$

Integrating,

$$\frac{1}{(1 - \alpha_1)\lambda} \ln \frac{2[-(1 - \alpha_1)]Y + (1 - \alpha_1)\lambda - (1 - \alpha_1)\lambda}{2[-(1 - \alpha_1)]Y + (1 - \alpha_1)\lambda + (1 - \alpha_1)\lambda} = n + c$$

$$\ln \frac{[-(1 - \alpha_1)]Y}{[-(1 - \alpha_1)]Y + (1 - \alpha_1)\lambda} = (1 - \alpha_1)n + c'$$

$$\ln \frac{-Y}{-Y + \lambda} = (1 - \alpha_1)\lambda n + c'.$$

20. A second possible approach is to find limits between which the average probability must lie and to inquire as to whether one of these limits can be used as an approximation to the average probability. If it is assumed that all individuals have the same parameters, it can be shown that (3-16) represents an upper bound on the average probability. See Bush and Mosteller, *op. cit.*, pp. 142–149.

21. H. S. Pearl and L. J. Reed, "On the Mathematical Theory of Growth," *Metron*, vol. 3, no. 1, 1923.

22. H. Martin and E. Reissner, *Elementary Differential Equations*, Addison-Wesley, Reading, Massachusetts, 1956, p. 34.

Raising both sides to e,

$$\frac{-Y}{\lambda - Y} = \exp\left[a_1 + (1 - \alpha_1)\lambda n\right]$$

$$-Y = (\lambda - Y)\exp\left[(1 - \alpha_1)\lambda n + a_1\right]$$

$$Y = Y\exp\left[(1 - \alpha_1)\lambda n + a_1\right] - \lambda\exp\left[(1 - \alpha_1)\lambda n + a_1\right]$$

$$Y - Y\exp\left[(1 - \alpha_1)\lambda n + a_1\right] = -\lambda\exp\left[(1 - \alpha_1)\lambda n + a_1\right]$$

$$\left\{1 - \exp\left[(1 - \alpha_1)\lambda n + a_1\right]\right\}Y = -\lambda\exp\left[(1 - \alpha_1)\lambda n + a_1\right]$$

$$Y = \frac{-\lambda\exp\left[(1 - \alpha_1)\lambda n + a_1\right]}{1 - \exp\left[(1 - \alpha_1)\lambda n + a_1\right]}$$

$$Y = \frac{\lambda\exp\left[(1 - \alpha_1)\lambda n + a_1\right]}{\left\{\exp\left[(1 - \alpha_1)\lambda n + a_1\right]\right\} - 1}$$

$$Y = \frac{\lambda}{1 - \exp\left[-a_1 - (1 - \alpha_1)\lambda n\right]}. \tag{3-17}$$

Thus, the value of the average response probability under the particular set of assumptions already outlined can be approximated as a logistic function of the number of trials the consumers have had. This is an equation form that has often appeared in discussions of sales increases of new consumer durable goods and of technological innovations. The application of this theory to durable goods will be discussed in detail in Chapter 5. The discussion of nondurable new-product innovation can now be completed.

Nondurable Innovation with Technical Substitutes

To this point it has been assumed that the new product has no close technical substitutes or complements. It seems sensible to inquire what happens when this assumption is untrue. Two different cases will be considered.

First, consider the case when $\lambda_2 = 0$, but $\alpha_2 \neq 1$. This case can be interpreted as the effect upon a successful new product of an unsuccessful technically competitive new product. In this case, the differential equation analogous to (3-16) is

$$\frac{dY}{dn} = [\lambda_1(1 - \alpha_1) + \alpha_2 - 1] - (\alpha_2 - \alpha_1)Y_n^2.$$

This is also a logistic equation, with the following solution:

$$Y = \frac{\dfrac{\lambda_1(1 - \alpha_1) + \alpha_2 - 1}{-(\alpha_1 - \alpha_2)}}{1 + \exp\left\{-a_0 - [\lambda_1(1 - \alpha_1) + \alpha_2 - 1]n\right\}}. \quad (3\text{-}18)$$

If (3-17) is assumed correct and (3-18) is in fact correct, two possible cases of bias in results are possible: First, if $\alpha_2 < \alpha_1$, the estimated rate of approach to equilibrium would have the wrong sign—a clear indication of failure of the proposed theory. Second, if $\alpha_2 > \alpha_1$ but $\alpha_2 \neq 1$, the rate of approach to equilibrium will appear higher than it actually is, and the derived estimate of λ_1 will typically be higher than λ_1 really is.

Next, consider the case when $\lambda_2 > 0$, and $\alpha_2 \neq 1.0$. This can be interpreted as arising from a situation in which another product is on the market that consumers conceive as a technical substitute for the supposedly new product. In this case the resulting differential equation is

$$\frac{dY}{dn} = \lambda_2(1 - \alpha_2) + [\lambda_1(1 - \alpha_1) - \lambda_2(1 - \alpha_2) + \alpha_2 - 1]Y$$

$$-(\alpha_2 - \alpha_1)Y^2. \quad (3\text{-}19)$$

This equation is readily soluble by previously given methods, but the solution is very cumbersome and is therefore not given here.[23] The effect of assuming (3-17) correct in this case is again clear. Typically, the rate of approach to equilibrium and the equilibrium probability will both be biased upward. However, in this case the fundamental equation form is different and thus a test may in principle be devised to discriminate between this case and the preceding ones. The next chapter will contain an illustration of one possible procedure.

This concludes the discussion of solutions that have been proposed to the aggregation problem. The reader will note, however, that the solutions proposed to this problem clarify an important remaining problem area. The question is, What factors affect the rate of learning in what way? This question will be studied empirically in Chapter 4 and reviewed in Chapter 5. It is of fundamental importance, but it should be noted that great theoretical progress has been made. From a state of considering a general, vague problem, the discussion has progressed to the point where very specific questions for future attention can be raised. It is now time to turn to a detailed discussion of the procedures and problems of bringing this theory face to face with data.

23. The solution has the form

$$Y = K_1 + K_2[(1 + K_3 e^{K_4 t})/(1 - K_3 e^{K_4 t})],$$

where the K's are appropriate functions of α_1, α_2, λ_1, and λ_2.

Chapter 4

Empirical Methods

This chapter will discuss in detail methods for estimating the parameters of the theory presented in the preceding chapters. The discussion naturally breaks into two parts: (1) use of panel data and (2) use of market data. It is amplified throughout whenever possible by use of actual data.

The use of data implies a focus on a particular situation in which consumer preferences may alter. The choice was made to pay particular attention to consumer response to new products. This choice can be defended on several grounds. First, it is clearly one of the important questions that the theory is capable of addressing. Second, it is a case in which the conditions outlined in Chapter 1 for the applicability of the theory are very likely to be met. Finally, data were available for this problem.

Panel Data

The analysis uses records of purchases of a nondurable product by reporting families belonging to a consumer panel. A typical consumer panel consists of a number of families who keep a chronological record of their purchases of food and household items. The panel provides data for each family, usually identified by a code number, on whether a purchase was made for each class of product (e.g., soap, canned green beans), on selected demographic characteristics of the family, such as family size, social class, and television ownership, and on the geographic market area in which the family resides. If a purchase is made, the brand purchased is reported; typically, the date, quantity, price, and store name relating to the purchase are also reported.[1]

Panel data provide a record of brand choices over an extended period of time. Such data should be quite clearly useful for application to the type of model outlined in the preceding chapters. Although such data are not perfect, studies of the accuracy of the data have shown that the errors are not so large as to render the data meaningless.[2]

The data utilized in this study were donated by a commercial company that operates a consumer panel with the permission of the companies who had originally purchased the data. For this reason, it is necessary not to reveal the geographic location of the market areas studied or the specific product or brands. Further, the data have been adjusted so as to ensure the preservation of these confidential facts. The adjustment is as follows: The data used relate only to panel members who were purchasers of the product class prior to the introduction of the new product. Since the product category is not purchased by all consumers, this

1. For a brief description of a particular panel (*Chicago Tribune*), see Ron Frank, "Brand Choice as a Probability Process," *Journal of Business*, vol. 35, no. 1, January, 1962.
2. Seymour Sudman, "On the Accuracy of Recording of Consumer Panels: I and II," *Journal of Marketing Research*, vol. I, nos. 2 and 3, respectively, 1964. These papers contain references to earlier studies of the same subject.

means the reported data cannot be used to generate an estimate of market sales, because they contain no information on entry by consumers (i.e., of the number of previous nonusers who became users because of the new product's introduction, or for whatever other reason). Finally, a word should be said about the quality of the quantity data. The product class is one of those in which the quantity measurement the product is sold by is different from the quantity measure applicable to measure consumption. For example, ice cream is sold by volume but consumed by weight. Two different quarts of ice cream may contain substantially different weights, and thus represent quite different amounts of consumption. For this reason, little use will be made of the quantity data.[3] Thus, the data are not in appropriate form to be used for all possible purposes. The sample is used in the sections that follow to illustrate methods and to provide an example of how inferences may be drawn from empirical work. These qualifications should not be forgotten in the following discussion, where for the sake of expositional ease the discussion will assume that the basic data is in appropriate form. Lastly, it should be noted the basic product is not perishable.

The data are for seven different geographic market areas for a twenty-four week period immediately following the introduction of the new product. Counting the new product, there were eight different brands available to consumers, although clearly not all stores would carry all eight brands. Data on distribution, i.e., the per cent of stores weighted by volume carrying each product, are not available. The total number of reporting families reporting all weeks is 1033. Table 4-1 summarizes the number of families purchasing the new product in each of the twenty-four weeks following its introduction. It can be seen that if the goal of the firm introducing the new product was to gain a large share of market, the new product was not particularly successful. However,

3. It should be noted that evidence indicates the consumption quantity of the product per quantity unit sold varies between brands and, indeed, even between packages of a given brand.

Table 4-1. Number of Families Purchasing New
Product by Time Period

Time Period	Number of Purchases	Time Period	Number of Purchases
1	5	13	2
2	4	14	8
3	6	15	2
4	6	16	6
5	2	17	4
6	5	18	1
7	2	19	4
8	3	20	8
9	2	21	8
10	6	22	7
11	4	23	8
12	4	24	7

several existing products had market shares about equal in terms of per cent of families to that established by the new product.

The fundamental question is, What do the data of Table 4-1 and the information Table 4-1 is derived from tell about the performance of the new product? To answer this question requires estimation techniques that can utilize the data to estimate the parameters of the model of consumer behavior. We now turn to consideration of this question.

Most discussions of parameter estimation techniques for models such as those under discussion rest on one of four techniques: the method of moments, least squares, minimum χ^2, and maximum likelihood. The discussion that follows will present examples of the use of each of these techniques.

Method of Moments

Strictly speaking, the method of moments involves deriving equations for the first k moments of a given distribution function and equating them to the appropriate observed sample moments. The desired estimates are then obtained by solving the resulting set of equations. It is known that such parameter estimates do not, in general, have the smallest possible variance in large samples.[4] Nevertheless, the method is often used because of practical expediency. Further, for some models used in learning theory, the method of moments yields parameter estimates that are also maximum likelihood estimates.[5] A modification of this method is sometimes used with regard to psychological models: Theoretical expressions and observed values of k statistics, which need not necessarily be the first k moments of the same distribution, are equated in order to estimate the parameters. A specific example of this modified method of moments will now be presented.

As has been stated, panel data give information on the sequence of trials, i.e., visits to stores to purchase goods, and on the action each consumer takes on each trial. The basic model of consumer response to new products presented in the previous chapter postulated a purchase operator

$$Q_1 p_t = \alpha_1 p_t + (1 - \alpha_1)\lambda_1$$

and a nonpurchase operator

$$Q_2 p_t = p_t.$$

From this it is possible to derive the distribution of the number of trials before the first purchase and between succeeding purchases. First the distribution of the number of trials, F_1, before the first purchase will be derived. The probability that the run is of length zero is $1 - q_0$, since this is the probability of purchasing on the

4. H. Cramer, *Mathematical Methods of Statistics*, Princeton University Press, Princeton, New Jersey, 1958, pp. 447–448.

5. For an example, see R. C. Atkinson, G. H. Bower, and E. J. Crothers, *An Introduction to Mathematical Learning Theory*, John Wiley & Sons, Inc., New York, 1965, chap. 2.

first trial after the new product is put on the market. The probability that the run is of length 1 is $q_0(1 - q_0)$, i.e., the probability that no purchase occurs on 0 but does occur on 1 (the consumer purchases on 1, after one no-purchase trial). Following this through, we obtain

$$Pr(F_1 = v) = q_0{}^v(1 - q_0).$$

The average length of a no-purchase run is simply $\mathscr{E}(F_1)$.

$$\mathscr{E}(F_1) = \sum_{v=0}^{\infty} vq_0{}^v(1 - q_0)$$

$$= \sum_{v=0}^{\infty} vq_0{}^v - \sum_{v=0}^{\infty} vq_0{}^{v+1}$$

$$= q_0\left(\sum_{v=0}^{\infty} vq_0{}^{v-1} - \sum_{v=0}^{\infty} vq_0{}^v\right).$$

Now,

$$\sum_{v=0}^{\infty} vq_0{}^{v-1} - \sum_{v=0}^{\infty} vq_0{}^v = 1 + q_0 + q_0{}^2 + q_0{}^3 + \cdots = \frac{1}{1 - q_0}.$$

It follows that

$$\mathscr{E}(F_1) = \frac{q_0}{p_0}. \qquad (4\text{-}1)$$

Further,

$$\sigma^2(F_1) = \mathscr{E}(F_1{}^2) - [\mathscr{E}(F_1)]^2$$

$$= \sum_{v=0}^{\infty} v^2 q_0{}^v(1 - q_0) - [\mathscr{E}(F_1)]^2$$

$$= \sum_{v=0}^{\infty} v^2 q_0{}^v - \sum_{v=0}^{\infty} v^2 q_0{}^{v+1} - [\mathscr{E}(F_1)]^2$$

$$= q_0\left(\sum_{v=0}^{\infty} v^2 q_0{}^{v-1} - \sum_{v=0}^{\infty} v^2 q_0{}^v\right) - [\mathscr{E}(F_1)]^2.$$

Now,

$$\sum_{v=0}^{\infty} v^2 q_0{}^{v-1} = 1 + 4q_0 + 9q_0{}^2 + 16q_0{}^3 + \cdots$$

and

$$\sum_{v=0}^{\infty} v^2 q_0{}^{v} = q_0 + 4q_0{}^2 + 9q_0{}^3 + 16q_0{}^4 + \cdots$$

so that

$$\sum_{v=0}^{\infty} v^2 q_0{}^{v-1} - \sum_{v=0}^{\infty} v^2 q_0{}^{v} = 1 + 3q_0 + 5q_0{}^2 + 7q_0{}^3 + 9q_0{}^4 + \cdots$$

Writing the above as the sum of two series,

$$\sum_{v=0}^{\infty} v^2 q_0{}^{v-1} - \sum_{v=0}^{\infty} v^2 q_0{}^{v} = 1 + q_0 + q_0{}^2 + q_0{}^3 + q_0{}^4 + \cdots$$

$$+ 2q_0 + 4q_0{}^2 + 6q_0{}^3 + 8q_0{}^4 + \cdots$$

$$= \frac{1}{1 - q_0}$$

$$+ 2(q_0 + 2q_0{}^2 + 3q_0{}^3 + 4q_0{}^4 + \cdots)$$

$$= \frac{1}{1 - q_0} + \frac{2q_0}{(1 - q_0)^2}.$$

Therefore,

$$\sigma^2(F_1) = q_0 \left(\frac{1}{1 - q_0} + \frac{2q_0}{(1 - q_0)^2} \right) - \left(\frac{q_0}{1 - q_0} \right)^2$$

$$= \frac{q_0(1 - q_0)}{(1 - q_0)^2} + \frac{2q_0{}^2}{(1 - q_0)^2} - \frac{q_0{}^2}{(1 - q_0)^2}$$

$$= \frac{q_0 - q_0{}^2 + 2q_0{}^2 - q_0{}^2}{(1 - q_0)^2}$$

so that

$$\sigma^2(F_1) = \frac{q_0}{(1 - q_0)^2}. \qquad (4\text{-}2)$$

When the consumer makes his first purchase the probabilities shift as follows:

$$p_1 = \alpha_1 p_0 + (1 - \alpha_1)\lambda_1$$
$$q_1 = (1 - p_1).$$

Assume that the consumer purchases on trial $n - 1$, with a no-purchase trial, of course, before this first purchase. Then a second no-purchase run begins on trial n. The probability that the run is of length zero is $1 - q_1$ since this is the probability of purchase on trial n. The probability that the run is of length 1 is $q_1(1 - q_1)$, i.e., the probability that no purchase occurs on trial n and that a purchase does occur on trial $n + 1$. Following this through as before:

$$\mathscr{E}(F_2) = \frac{q_1}{p_1} \qquad \text{and} \qquad \sigma^2(F_2) = \frac{q_1}{(1 - q_1)^2}.$$

Suppose the consumer purchases again; then

$$
\begin{aligned}
p_2 &= \alpha_1 p_1 + (1 - \alpha_1)\lambda_1 \\
    &= \alpha_1[\alpha_1 p_0 + (1 - \alpha_1)\lambda_1] + (1 - \alpha_1)\lambda_1 \\
    &= \alpha_1^2 p_0 + \alpha_1 \lambda_1 - \alpha_1^2 \lambda_1 + \lambda_1 - \alpha_1 \lambda_1 \\
    &= \alpha_1^2 p_0 + (1 - \alpha_1^2)\lambda_1 \\
q_2 &= 1 - p_2.
\end{aligned}
$$

Similarly,

$$\mathcal{E}(F_3) = \frac{q_2}{p_2} \quad \text{and} \quad \sigma^3(F_3) = \frac{q_2}{(1 - q_2)^2}.$$

Analysis of this type may be continued as long as desired, of course.

The parameters of the basic model may be estimated by fitting moments. This may not be, of course, an efficient estimation method. Moreover, in the actual handling of the data some bias may be introduced because there must be a cut-off made to estimate the parameters at a given point in time. However, this method has the advantage that it may provide a quick and useful way to get rough estimates of parameter values to be used in policy decisions that must be quickly made.

Assuming that the product remains on the market and the firm pursues a stable marketing policy, $\mathcal{E}(F_n)$ should become constant as n becomes quite large. This is because the model implies that a stable probability of purchase is approached under conditions of this type. · That is, the purchase probability in aggregate, and for any given family, would remain constant at equilibrium. It could not be said that the result of a stable probability in such cases would "cast suspicion on the use of a learning 'model' to describe the observations."[6] The results (4-1), (4-2), etc. clearly allow estimation of the parameters of the model, given appropriate data. Since panel data are recorded weekly, a week will be the basic unit of time. The summary statistics necessary for the estimation of parameters are presented in Table 4-2.

Using the data on all panel members of (F_1), we obtain

$$\mathcal{E}(F_1) = \frac{q_0}{p_0} = 23.3 \Rightarrow p_0 = \frac{1}{24.3} = 0.041$$

6. Frank, *op. cit.*

Table 4-2. Summary Statistics for Method-of-Moments Parameter Estimation

	All Data	Data for Purchasers only			
	$1^\dagger$	1	2	3	4
Number of purchasers	1045	60	19	8	6
Number of weeks to purchase number	24,305	761	94	36	14
Average number of weeks to purchase number	23.3	12.5	4.9	4.5	2.3
Variance of number of weeks to purchase number	10.8	67.8	29.3	36.8	3.1
Standard deviation of number of weeks to purchase number	3.3	8.2	5.4	6.1	1.8

† No purchase = 24 weeks; includes all families who were panel members at the start of the 24-week period.

$$\mathscr{E}(F_2) = \frac{q_1}{p_1} = 4.9 \Rightarrow p_1 = \frac{1}{5.9} = 0.170$$

$$\mathscr{E}(F_3) = \frac{q_2}{p_2} = 4.5 \Rightarrow p_2 = \frac{1}{5.5} = 0.182$$

$$p_1 = \alpha_1 p_0 + (1 - \alpha_1)\lambda_1$$

$$p_2 = \alpha_1 p_1 + (1 - \alpha_1)\lambda_1.$$

All that is necessary is to substitute in the estimated values of $p_0, p_1,$ and p_2, and solve the resulting equation to obtain an estimate of α_1 and λ_1. When these operations are performed, $\lambda_1 = 0.130$ and $\alpha_1 = -0.45$. Although a negative α_1 is possible theoretically, as long as it is between 0 and -1, it is surprising because it implies oscillatory behavior. This is not at all what would be expected on the basis of common sense. The same calculations, using the figures for purchasers only $\mathscr{E}(F_1)$, yield $p_0 = 0.074, \alpha_1 = 0.119$, and $\lambda_1 = 0.183$. Finally, the same calculations, using the buyers-only figures for $\mathscr{E}(F_2)$, $\mathscr{E}(F_3)$, $\mathscr{E}(F_4)$, with $p_3 = 0.303$, yields $\alpha_1 = 10.2$, and $\lambda_1 = 0.169$. This is simply not a sensible value for α_1. The results are collected in Table 4-3.

Table 4-3

Data Used	α_1	λ_1	p_0
All F_1, F_2, F_3	-0.045	0.130	0.041
Buyers F_1, F_2, F_3	0.119	0.183	0.074
Buyers only F_2, F_3, F_4	10.2	0.169	

The general feeling these results give is one of suspicion that they are not reasonable. There is a good reason for this: the possibility of serious truncation error. Table 4-2 shows that out of 1045 families reporting at week 1, only 60 purchased the new product at least once. For the other 981 families, the number of weeks to first purchase is arbitrarily set at 24. This procedure surely yields a great truncation error. The alternative is to ignore the 981 families; this should have the effect of biasing upward the estimates of the learning rate α and the asymptotic aggregate probability of purchase λ. Using the procedure on data for second purchase, third purchase, and so on, must involve similar problems.

The data to which this method has been successfully applied by psychologists is quite different in that there is typically little, if any, truncation error. It is usually a simple matter to run a learning experiment in a laboratory until all subjects have made the desired response several times. This is not the case with the present data. Conversely, this argument would lead to the suspicion that the method of moments should work reasonably well for a new product tried by many people quite rapidly;

this might be the case, for example, if the new product were widely sampled. The problem to investigate is how other proposed estimation procedures react to this set of data. Perhaps, although it is clearly an optimistic position, some other estimation procedure will give parameter estimates with better face validity.

Least Squares[7]

It has been previously shown that the subject-controlled learning theory predicts a linear relation between probability of purchasing at the previous time and at the present time. The particular values the parameters assume depend upon whether the product is purchased or not. Because of the linear operator assumption, it should be possible to estimate the parameters of the learning model directly by application of modified least-squares methods to the resulting linear equations. In the case of a new product, this should be of particular interest because, intuitively speaking, it might be possible to use such methods to construct a test of the hypothesis that the rejection operator for new products has zero intercept and unitary slope.

Recently James M. Carman has proposed a method of estimating the parameters of the basic learning model (3-1) and (3-2) from panel data.[8] In Carman's notation, the model is

$$\text{Purchase operator} = P_{p,t+1} = \alpha_p + \beta P_t \qquad (4\text{-}3)$$
$$\text{Rejection operator} = P_{R,t+1} = \alpha_R + \beta P_t,$$

where α_p, α_R, and β are the parameters to be estimated. The slopes of both operators are assumed to be equal, and P_t, $P_{p,t+1}$, and

7. This section of this chapter has been coauthored by Richard L. Baumann.

8. The basic reference is James M. Carman, "Brand Switching and Linear Learning Models: Some Empirical Results," Working Paper no. 20, Research Program in Marketing, Graduate School of Business Administration, University of California, Berkeley, California, August 6, 1965. A version of this paper has been published in the *Journal of Advertising Research*, June, 1966. The derivation of the estimation procedure has unfortunately been excluded from the reprinted article.

$P_{R,t+1}$ are probabilities of consumers buying a particular brand on trial t, probability of purchase on trial $t + 1$, given purchase on t, and probability of purchase on trial $t + 1$ given rejection, i.e., nonpurchase, on trial t, respectively.

The present data stand in sharp contrast to the data Carman used. Carman had a large panel sample (5028 families); the present data 1045 families have a sample size about one-fifth the size of Carman's sample. The product Carman studied, Crest toothpaste, was an extremely successful product during the period used in the analysis, which was immediately after endorsement in August of 1960 by the Council of Dental Therapeutics of the American Dental Association. The product under study here appears not to have been very widely used. This causes a straightforward replication of Carman's techniques to be difficult and necessitates a modification of his analysis.

Carman first segregated the families in his panel by the average purchase interval between purchases of toothpaste. He then constructed trees of purchase sequences for each group and used these to compute the conditional probability of being in a particular branch from the relative frequencies of people in each branch. The paucity of purchasers for the current product precluded a breakdown by average interval of purchase; therefore, all purchases were used without regard to the interval between them. Applying this technique to the data yielded the tree of purchase sequences illustrated in Figure 4-1. The branches of the tree are carried out as far as they are useful in the analysis. Using this tree makes it possible to determine the probability of purchase in a given period P_t and the two probabilities of purchasing in the following period, given either a purchase of a nonpurchase in period t. Thus, Figure 4-1 shows 1045 consuming families entering the tree. Of these 1045, twelve purchased the new product on their first purchase and 1033 did not. Thus at $t = 1$, the probability of this group's purchasing the new product is $^{12}/_{1045} = .015 = P_t$. Of the 12 who did purchase, 4 again bought the new product on their next purchase occasion, and 8 did not.

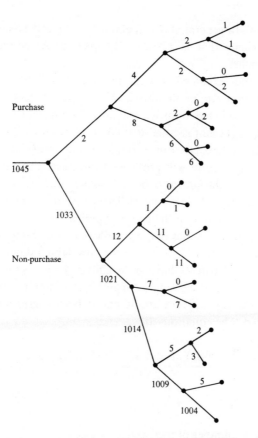

FIGURE 4-1. Branching Tree for Product. Upper branch is always purchase; lower branch is always non-purchase.

Thus $P_{P,t+1}$ at $t = 1$ is $\frac{4}{12} = .333$. Of the 1033 who did not purchase the new product at $t = 1$, 12 did so on the next purchase occasion. Thus $P_{R,t+1}$ at $t = 1$ is $\frac{12}{1033} = .016$. This yields one set of observations, a single conditional probability triplet, used to estimate the parameters of the model. This triplet provides one point $(P_t, P_{p,t+1})$ for estimating the purchase operator and one point $(P_t, P_{R,t+1})$ for estimating the rejection operator. From Figure 4-1, four more triplets can be similarly derived (see

Table 4-4). In general, if Q is the number of purchases, a tree can be constructed that has $(2^{Q-1}) - 1$ triplets, provided there are no null branches.

Carman excluded triplets containing null branches from consideration for computation of the parameters. The logic underlying this has intuitive meaning. Saying that a $(P_t, P_{P,t+1})$ or $(P_t, P_{R,t+1})$ point is equal to 1.00 or .00 is illogical for making population inferences. For example, a probability of 1.00 or .00 that the population will purchase a product, given that it was purchased in the previous period, makes little sense when the population as a whole is viewed. This convention of ignoring null branches is followed in the present application.

Carman also states that he employed a weighting scheme on his data.[9] The present analysis uses unweighted data.

When all triplets have been collected, the parameters are estimated by a least-squares regression technique, where the sum of the squared deviations about both regression lines is minimized. The equations are

$$\hat{\beta} = \frac{N(\Sigma Y_P X + \Sigma Y_R X) - \Sigma X(\Sigma Y_R + \Sigma Y_P)}{2N\Sigma X^2 - 2(\Sigma X)^2}$$

$$\hat{\alpha}_p = \overline{Y}_p - \hat{\beta}\overline{X} \qquad \text{and} \qquad \hat{\alpha}_R = \overline{Y}_R - \hat{\beta}\overline{X},$$

where N = number of triplets
$X = P_t$
$Y_p = P_{p,t+1}$
$Y_R = P_{R,t+1}$

9. He describes the weighting scheme as follows: "... the observations were weighted by the number of consumers at time t divided by the number of levels of branches in the tree. The result of this weighting scheme is that an observation triplet is weighted by the number of consumers who generated that triplet, but the sum of the weights is approximately equal to the number of consumers in the tree." The use of weights presumes the sample size is not proportional to the population size. Weighted data yield $\alpha_1 = \alpha_2 = 0.335$, $\lambda_1 = 0.0812$, $\lambda_2 = 0.00183$, and $R^2 = .01$. I am indebted to James Carman for an explanation of the weighting procedure.

$\overline{Y}_p$ = average value of $P_{p,t+1}$
$\overline{Y}_R$ = average value of $P_{R,t+1}$
$\overline{X}$ = average value of P_t.

Table 4-4 tabulates the basic data used in the computation. Using this data with the program given in Appendix B, the following results are achieved:[10]

$$\beta = 0.7130, \qquad \alpha_P = 0.2535, \qquad \alpha_R = 0.0125.$$

Table 4-4. Data Used in Computation

$X_t = P_t$	$Y_P = P_{p,t+1}$	$Y_R = P_{R,t+1}$
$^{12}/_{1045}$ = .015	$^{4}/_{12}$ = .333	$^{12}/_{1033}$ = .016
$^{4}/_{12}$ = .333	$^{2}/_{4}$ = .500	$^{2}/_{8}$ = .250
$^{12}/_{1033}$ = .016	$^{1}/_{12}$ = .083	$^{7}/_{1021}$ = .0068
$^{5}/_{1014}$ = .0049	$^{2}/_{5}$ = .400	$^{5}/_{1009}$ = .0050
$^{2}/_{5}$ = .400	$^{1}/_{2}$ = .500	$^{1}/_{3}$ = .333

First these results should be displayed in a form compatible with the previous discussion. Carman uses β for the slope (α has been previously used), and α for the intercept (a is the previous notation). Performing this computation, where $\lambda = a/1 - \alpha$, the following results are obtained:

$$\alpha_p = \alpha_R = 0.7130, \qquad \lambda_p = 0.886, \qquad \lambda_R = 0.0435.$$

Interpretation of the meaningfulness of these results is not easy. The rejection operation has almost a zero intercept. The calculation procedure requires the slope of the two operators to be the same. If, in fact, the rejection operator did have a zero intercept

10. One can compute an R^2 and a significance test on the R^2. A program is also given in Appendix B for this calculation. Performing this calculation, $R^2 = 0.22$, which is not significant at $\alpha = 0.05$ (three degrees of freedom). However, such a test depends upon the usual assumptions about the nature of the error term, which may be inappropriate in this context.

and unit slope, one could expect that use of the Carman procedure would result in an estimate of the slope that would be biased upward toward 1. It must be recalled that the Carman procedure was devised for use with old products in which such a forcing assumption might not be too seriously incorrect.

An effort may be made to check the above conjecture. If, in fact, the rejection operator has a zero intercept and unit slope, then there should be a linear relation between the aggregate probability of purchase at times t and $t + 1$. Table 4-5 tabulates unbiased estimates of P_t and P_{t-1} to be used in an ordinary least-squares regression.[11]

Table 4-5. Input Data for Ordinary Least-Squares
Estimates of Purchase Operator Parameters

Obs. No.	$P_t \times 10^2$	$P_{t-1} \times 10^2$	Obs. No.	$P_t \times 10^2$	$P_{t-1} \times 10^2$
01	.2907	.3876	13	.6783	.0969
02	.4845	.2907	14	.0969	.6783
03	.4845	.4845	15	.4845	.0969
04	.0969	.4845	16	.2907	.4845
05	.3876	.0969	17	.0000	.2907
06	.0969	.3876	18	.2907	.0000
07	.1938	.0969	19	.6783	.2907
08	.0969	.1938	20	.6783	.6783
09	.4845	.0969	21	.5814	.6783
10	.2907	.4845	22	.6783	.5814
11	.2907	.2907	23	.5814	.6783
12	.0969	.2907			

The results of this regression are

$$\alpha_p = 0.3085, \qquad \beta_p = 0.1486, \qquad R = 0.1486.$$

By assumption, $\alpha_R = 0$ and $\beta_R = 1$. The implied value of λ is

11. These are the same numbers used in the next section (minimum X^2, estimates) where their derivation is presented.

0.00359. Note that this value of λ has been back-adjusted for the input-data adjustment.

The value of the intercept of the purchase operator is not much different from that derived by use of Carman's method; but the value of β_p is much less. The regression is not significant at $\alpha = 0.05$. The much lower value for β_p is consistent with the conjecture, but the lack of significance of the regression precludes drawing any strong conclusions.

One central problem with least squares as applied to this problem is that the least-squares estimation procedure is not also a maximum-likelihood procedure. The likelihood function to be given later will make this very clear. The result is that it is very difficult to evaluate the results. The question of the meaningfulness of these results must be deferred until they can be compared with results from other estimation procedures.

Minimum χ^2 Estimates

This section returns to the basic new-product model for its hypothesis.

$$
\begin{aligned}
Q_1 p_t &= \alpha_1 p_t + (1 - \alpha_1)\lambda_1 \\
Q_2 p_t &= p_t
\end{aligned}
\tag{4-4}
$$

Given this hypothesis, it follows that after a product has been purchased V times its probability of purchase is

$$
p_V = Q_1{}^V p_0 = \alpha_1{}^V p_0 + (1 - \alpha_1{}^V)\lambda_1.
$$

Still assuming that all families in the panel have the same parameter values, on the Vth trial N_V families purchase. Let there be N_0 families in the panel. Then

$$
\hat{p}_V = \frac{N_V - 1}{N_0 - 1}
$$

is an unbiased estimate of p_V;[12] and

$$\sigma^2(\hat{p}) \cong \frac{p_V{}^2(1 - p_V)}{X_V}.$$

Then the following expression may be written:

$$\chi^2 = \sum_{V=0}^{\Omega} \frac{(p_V - \hat{p}_V)^2}{\sigma^2(\hat{p}_V)}$$

$$= \sum_{V=0}^{\Omega} W_V[\alpha_1{}^V p_0 + (1 - \alpha_1{}^V)\lambda_1 - \hat{p}_V]^2, \quad (4\text{-}5)$$

where $W_V = 1/\sigma^2(p_V)$, and Ω is the largest number of trials used for estimation purposes.[13]

Bush and Mosteller suggest minimizing the chi-square like quantity (4-5) as a method of estimating the parameters of (4-4). Since such a procedure also yields a value of χ^2, it provides a means of testing the null hypothesis that the variation in observed data can be explained by the model (4-4). Equation (4-5) employs data that are usually available from consumer panels.

To obtain the minimizing equations, Bush and Mosteller argue that the W's may be regarded as weights and may thus be assumed constant as a first approximation. The minimizing equations may then be obtained by differentiating (4-5) partially with respect to p_0, λ_1, and α_1, and setting the results equal to zero. Performing this differentiation, Bush and Mosteller obtain from p_0, λ_1, and α_1, respectively,

$$\sum_V W_V \alpha_1{}^V [\alpha_1{}^V p_0 + (1 - \alpha_1{}^V)\lambda_1 - \hat{p}_V] = 0 \quad (4\text{-}6)$$

$$\sum_V W_V (1 - \alpha_1{}^V)[\alpha_1{}^V p_0 + (1 - \alpha_1{}^V)\lambda_1 - \hat{p}_V] = 0 \quad (4\text{-}7)$$

    12. See M. A. Girshick, F. Mosteller, and L. J. Savage, "Unbiased Estimates for Certain Binomial Sampling Problems with Applications," *Annals of Mathematical Statistics*, vol. 17, 1946, pp. 13–23.
    13. Bush and Mosteller, *op. cit.*, p. 231.

$$\sum_V W_V V \alpha_1^{V-1} [\alpha_1^V p_0 + (1 - \alpha_1^V)\lambda_1 - \hat{p}_V] = 0. \quad \textbf{(4-8)}$$

The computations then proceed as follows: First assume all weights are constant. Choose a value for α_1. Then solve (4-6) and (4-7) for λ_1 and p_0. Substitute the parameter values in (4-8), and see if the result is zero. If not, repeat the procedure until a result of approximately zero for the value of (4-8) is obtained. This yields preliminary working values for the three parameters. A computer program for this first step is given in Appendix C.

The next step is to use these preliminary parameter values to compute weights and to repeat the direct search procedure already outlined with the unequal weights. Then the set of parameter values is used to calculate new weights, and the process is repeated until the parameter values become stable. The final set of weights may then be used to compute an empirical value for χ^2. A computer program for this step is also given in Appendix C. Table 4-6 tabulates the values of $\hat{p}_V$ derived from the panel data to be used in estimating the parameters of (4-2).

Table 4-6. Input Data for Minimum χ^2 Estimation of Parameters of Eq. (4-2)

V	$\hat{p}_V$	V	$\hat{p}_V$
0	.003876	12	.000969
1	.002907	13	.006783
2	.004845	14	.000969
3	.004845	15	.004845
4	.000969	16	.002907
5	.003876	17	.000000
6	.000969	18	.002907
7	.001938	19	.006783
8	.000969	20	.006783
9	.004845	21	.005814
10	.002907	22	.006783
11	.002907	23	.005814

The direct search procedure, which assumes constant weights, yields the following answers: $\alpha_1 = 0.325$, $p_0 = .00376$, $\lambda_1 = 0.00362$. Then the second step is performed of allowing the weights to vary and of iteratively searching for a stable answer. The step-by-step input and answers from this second step are tabulated in Table 4-7. The final results are $\alpha_1 = 0.319$, $p_0 = .00363$, $\lambda_1 = 0.00654$. It can be seen that only the value of λ_1 is much different from the constant-weight answer, and even this value is of a similar order of magnitude. The observed χ^2 value for these parameters is 18.13; $\chi^2_{(21)}$ at $\alpha = 0.05 = 32.7$. Therefore, the null hypothesis that the observations fit the data cannot be rejected.

The previous low R^2 values reported in the least-squares section of this chapter cannot be taken as contradictory evidence. It was pointed out there (but this will surely bear repetition) that the assumptions necessary to use the usual significance test on R^2 are not met. What this result does point out is that ignoring the

Table 4-7. Input and Answers, by Step, of Weighted Minimum χ^2 Computations

Run No.	Start	Answer Minimum Residual Value for (4-6)
1	$\alpha_1 = 0.325$ $P_0 = .00376$ $\lambda_1 = 0.00362$	$\alpha_1 = 0.140$ $P_0 = .00181$ $\lambda_1 = 0.00640$
2	$\alpha_1 = 0.140$ $P_0 = .00181$ $\lambda_1 = 0.00640$	$\alpha_1 = 0.315$ $P_0 = .384$ $\lambda_1 = 0.00653$
3	$\alpha_1 = 0.315$ $P_0 = .00384$ $\lambda_1 = 0.00653$	$\alpha_1 = 0.319$ $P_0 = .00363$ $\lambda_1 = 0.00654$

Note: Final answer is that achieved as output on run 3; initial starting parameters derived from constant weight assumption calculations.

fact that the R^2 generated by applying least squares to the model should be routinely tested for significance could lead to very misleading conclusions being drawn. Further, the value of λ computed by ordinary least-squares estimates was 0.00359, which is quite close to the estimate derived from the constant-weight minimum χ^2 technique. However, the α_1 value (0.1486) is substantially lower than that found with the minimum χ^2 technique.

Maximum Likelihood

This section discusses the possibility of obtaining maximum-likelihood estimates of the parameters of the basic model of consumer behavior. This problem has also been studied by W. F. Massy, but the approach in this section will differ from that taken by him.[14] Massy attempts to solve both the aggregation problem and the maximum-likelihood-estimation problem. In this section, the solution proposed to the aggregation problem in Chapter 3 will be taken as a base point, and the possibility of obtaining maximum-likelihood estimates discussed with this solution in mind. The previous section has shown that the model cannot be rejected according to the minimum χ^2 estimation technique. Surely one question to pose is whether this technique apparently leads to parameter estimates identical with those derived from maximizing a likelihood function.

The basic model is, once again,

$$Q_1 p = \alpha_1 p + (1 - \alpha_1)\lambda_1$$
$$Q_2 p = p.$$

As before, when the new product has been purchased exactly V times, its probability of purchase has reached

$$p_V = Q_1{}^V p_0 = \alpha_1{}^V p_0 + (1 - \alpha_1{}^V)\lambda_1 .$$

---

14. F. Massy, "Estimation of Parameters for Linear Learning Models," Working Paper no. 78, Graduate School of Business, Stanford University, Stanford, California, October, 1965.

For each value of V, there exists a number of observations concerning whether or not alternative A_j occurred. These observations will be from a number of different families in the present context. Let the number of observations for a specified value of V be N_V, and use the index μ to denote these N_V observations, that is, $\mu = 1, 2, \ldots, N_V$. The μth observation for a particular value of V is simply whether A_j occurred or not. Represent the data by a set of random variables, $X_{\mu V}$.

Let A_j = nonpurchase of the new product
$X_{\mu V} = 0$ if A_j occurred
$X_{\mu V} = 1$ if A_j did not occur.

The data are thereby reduced to a set of 0's and 1's. Let

$$X_V = \sum_{\mu = 1}^{N_V} X_{\mu V}.$$

Therefore, X_V is the number of times A_j did not occur on N_V observations, since a zero is entered in the sum when A_j occurs and a one when A_j does not occur. The number of occurrences of A_j during the N_V observations is, of course, $N_V - X_V$. The data give the value of all the $X_{\mu V}$'s, and from those volumes maximum-likelihood estimates of p_0, α_1, and λ_1 may be determined in principle.[15] The likelihood function is

$$\mathscr{L} = \prod_{V = 0}^{\Omega} [(p_V)^{X_V}(1 - p_V)^{N_V - X_V}]$$

$$= \prod_{V = 0}^{\Omega} \left\{ [\alpha_1{}^V p_0 + (1 - \alpha_1{}^V)\lambda_1]^{X_V} \{1 - [\alpha_1{}^V p_0 + (1 - \alpha_1{}^V)\lambda_1]\}^{N_V - X_V} \right\}$$

---

15. H. Cramer, *Mathematical Methods of Statistics*, Princeton University Press, Princeton, New Jersey, 1955, contains a discussion of the maximum-likelihood principle in general.

The natural logarithm of $\mathscr{L}$ is

$$\ln \mathscr{L} = \sum_{V=0}^{\Omega} \bigg(X_V \ln \left[a_1{}^V p_0 + (1 - \alpha_1{}^V)\lambda_1 \right]$$
$$+ (N_V - X_V) \ln \left\{ 1 - [\alpha_1{}^V p_0 + (1 - \alpha_1{}^V)\lambda_1] \right\} \bigg).$$

This expression is not very tractable analytically but for given values of α_1, p_0, and λ_1 may readily be evaluated numerically, given a set of data. A computer program to perform this evaluation is given in Appendix D.

The basic data to be used has already been presented in Table 4-1. The V index is one less than the time-period index given in Table 4-1. Applying these data to the likelihood function for a set of values of α_1, p_0, and λ_1 yielded results shown in Table 4-8.

In Table 4-8, the first two sets of parameters are, respectively, the results of the unweighted and weighted minimum χ^2 estimation technique. The following parameter sets were chosen to investigate the hypothesis that the weighted minimum χ^2 estimation technique produced at least a local maxima of the likelihood function. The calculated values of the likelihood function that

Table 4-8. Values of Natural Logarithm of $\mathscr{L}$, Given
Data of Table 4-1 and Parameter Values Shown

Parameter Values

p_0	α_1	λ_1	$\ln \mathscr{L}$
.0376	0.325	0.00362	-759.442
.00363	0.319	0.00654	-734.849
.00360	0.319	0.00654	-734.855
.00369	0.319	0.00654	$-734.835*$
.00363	0.320	0.00654	-734.847
.00363	0.318	0.00654	-734.849
.00363	0.319	0.00659	-734.194
.00363	0.319	0.00650	$-734.575*$
.00360	0.315	0.00650	$-734.549*$

appear to disprove this hypothesis are marked with an asterisk. Thus it would appear that the hypothesis that the weighted minimum χ^2 estimation procedure is also maximum likelihood cannot be maintained.[16]

Recently, Kuehn, Weiss, and McGuire have also reported results on using direct search methods to obtain maximum likelihood estimates of the parameters of equation (3-6).[17] They report that this procedure can be readily used to derive parameter estimates. The problem with such a procedure, of course, is that it does not generate a measure of goodness to fit. However, such a procedure could be readily adapted to the likelihood function if a direct-search program were available.

Concluding Comments

This concludes a review and discussion of several methods of analyzing panel data, given the basic dynamic model of consumer behavior developed in the first three chapters of this book. As an overview, it has been seen that estimation based on the method of moments is likely to be of little value compared to other methods, and that the weighted minimum χ^2 technique has much to commend it, including a measure of the goodness of fit of the model to data. We are now ready to proceed with a discussion of using market data to attempt to subject the theory to test.[18]

16. Of course, it might be objected that not enough iterations were performed in the minimum χ^2 technique. Although this may be true, it is also true the iterations were halted when stable parameter values were obtained, which is when it seems sensible to halt. The conjecture here appears the more reasonable explanation to me, although it is surely one which should be subjected to further study.

17. Alfred A. Kuehn, Timothy W. McGuire, and Doyle L. Weiss, "Measuring the Effectiveness of Advertising," in Raymond M. Haas, ed., *Science, Technology and Marketing*, American Marketing Association, 230 N. Michigan Avenue, Chicago, Ilinois, January, 1967, pp. 185–194. The model they use defined the value of advertising as a stock of goodwill derived from past advertising expenditures weighted by their effectiveness and adjusted for the decay in goodwill so obtained over time. The model is in all other respects simply that explicated in the first section of Chapter 3 of this book.

18. This next section draws heavily on the author's "A Theory of Market Behavior After Innovation," *Management Science*, July, 1964, and is reproduced with permission of *Management Science*.

Estimation from Market Data

Aggregate market data are usually terms of sales and data on the firm's marketing strategy. This section will discuss the use of the model presented to such data.

Data that deal with a market area must represent an average of individual decisions within the market. As was previously discussed in Chapter 3, the equation for average probabilities over trials, or time, is

$$\frac{dY}{dt} = (1 - \alpha_1)\lambda Y - (1 - \alpha)Y^2$$

Market data are in terms of sales. The first problem is one of going from probability of purchase to sales. This can be done by first multiplying the purchase probability by the population in the area N_0 to get an expected number of families and then multiplying the expected number of families by a hypothetical purchase size Q per purchasing family. The resulting equation, where X represents sales for a given time period, is

$$\frac{dX}{dt} = (1 - \alpha_1)LX - (1 - \alpha_1)X^2 \qquad \textbf{(4-9)}$$

$$L = \lambda_1(N_0)(Q).$$

L, of course, represents the asymptote sales approach during the introductory period. It is the maximum expected number of families purchasing times the hypothetical purchase size. Again, α is simply a measure of the rate at which the asymptote is approached.

There is a large literature on the estimation problems of equations like (4-9). We shall adopt an estimation procedure described by Tintner[19] because it yields estimates of the two parameters which are most important, L and $1 - \alpha$.

19. G. Tintner, *Econometrics*, John Wiley & Sons, Inc., New York, 1952, pp. 208ff.

The procedure is as follows. First rewrite (4-9) as

$$\frac{1}{X}\frac{dX}{dt} = (1 - \alpha)L - (1 - \alpha)X.$$

If the interval of time is not too large,

$$\frac{1}{X}\frac{dX}{dt} = \frac{\Delta X}{X} = \frac{X_{t+1} - X_t}{X_t} = R(t),$$

and

$$R(t) = (1 - \alpha)L - (1 - \alpha)X_t$$

or

$$\Delta X_t = (1 - \alpha)X_t(L - X_t). \qquad (\textbf{4-10})$$

Equation (4-10) may be fitted by least squares.

If cross-sectional data over many markets exist, along with supporting data on the firm's marketing actions, then one can investigate the effects of the firm's marketing actions on the asymptotic sales level and the rate of approach to this asymptotic sales level and the rate of approach to this asymptote. As a working hypothesis, the rate of approach to the asymptote may be thought to be determined by the initial actions of the firm, i.e., by the price, income, promotions, advertising, availability, and product characteristics during the early stages of the introductory period. It is hypothesized that the asymptote is determined by the effect of these variables throughout the entire introductory period. The next section will present some empirical results and an evaluation and discussion of them.

A Discussion of Some Data

The available data represent data on sales of a new product in quantity. These sales data are given in sales per two months. Accompanying this are auxiliary data on the availability of the good at the retail level, dollars spent by the company on promotions, and dollars spent by the company on advertising. No data were available on the price of the good, other than an assertion by the company that price was held constant throughout the introductory period in all regions. Data on product characteristics and consumer income were also not available. The auxiliary data are not available for all the markets for which sales data are available; complete sales data on all markets are not available. Only the data that are complete are used.

Since the sales data are given on a two-month basis, it is important to note one thing. An event has previously been defined as a consumer's trip to the supermarket, which may be thought to occur about once a week. The effect of this disparity between time and event (that is, that up to eight events may occur within one time period) will be to decrease the apparent estimate of $1 - \alpha$. As long as the number of events within a time period remains constant, there should be no other effect on the parameter estimates. For example, suppose there are eight such events in a two-month period, and the empirical estimate of $1 - \alpha$ is 0.000356. The corresponding estimate of $1 - \alpha$ that would be expected to be derived from weekly purchase-panel data would be $\sqrt[8]{.00356} = 0.370$.

Data for one marketing region for another product are also available. First, we test the previous theory using the market sales data. Recall that the equation being estimated is

$$R(t) = \frac{1}{X} \frac{dX}{dt} = (1 - \alpha)L - (1 - \alpha)X.$$

By estimating this equation, the results in Table 4-9 are obtained.

The data terminate at the end of the introductory period, as defined by the company providing the data. Their definition was that this should be one year after the company first promoted and advertised the product.

Two of these thirty-four regions are not significant at a type-one error of 0.10. Since the type-one error is one of rejecting a hypothesis when it is actually true, it can be seen that an apparent insignificance of two out of thirty-four regions is consistent with this if a fiducial probability viewpoint is adopted. However, even if such a view is not adopted, the theory seems to be consistent with the data in general at $\alpha = 0.10$, with the two exceptions noted above.

Now we seek to relate the estimated parameters to the marketing actions of the firm. Before doing this, it is important to realize that in some of the regions a certain amount of sales is made before the firm makes any other marketing actions, i.e., before the firm begins to promote, advertise, and seek to place the product in the stores in the area. These sales stem from stores stocking the good because other stores of the same chain carry the good in a different marketing area.

If a correct picture of the effect of the firm's marketing actions on sales is to be reached, these early sales should be eliminated from the data. Another variable—availability of the good before the good is promoted and advertised—can then be introduced in an effort to show the effect of such prior availability of the good on the parameters thus estimated. Thus a second set of regressions was run from the data, with the data adjusted by the deletion of these early sales. Table 4-10 presents the results arising from the adjusted data.

Comparison of these results with those of Table 4-9 reveals that the estimates of L are essentially the same, and that the estimates of $1 - \alpha$ in Table 4-2 are generally smaller than those of Table 4-9. So far as the statistical significance of the results is concerned, it is essentially the same as found in Table 4-9.

It is now possible to make an inquiry into the effect of the firm's marketing policy on the value of the parameters $1 - \alpha$ and L. The estimated parameters are assumed to be linear functions of the independent variable.

Table 4-9. Basic Data Results

Product	Region	$1 - \alpha$	L	F	$n_1 n_2$	Significance Level	
1	1	0.0242	2,418	12.98	1,8	+	($\alpha = 0.01$)
2	1	0.000446	14,074	6.56	1,6	*	($\alpha = 0.05$)
	2	0.00174	4,534	21.09	1,5	+	
	3	0.0268	4,348	2.54	1,6		
	4	0.00606	4,843	23.05	1,5	+	
	5	0.00391	4,430	12.09	1,5	*	
	6	0.00857	4,006	5.83	1,6	0	($\alpha = 0.10$)
	7	0.00340	3,197	9.09	1,6	*	
	8	0.000921	2,801	2.26	1,8		
	9	0.00336	3,414	5.36	1,7	0	
	10	0.00140	3,097	4.26	1,8	0	
	11	0.00399	2,386	35.72	1,6	+	
	12	0.00409	2,738	11.10	1,5	*	
	13	0.00287	3,906	12.63	1,5	*	
	14	0.00408	5,400	11.01	1,5	*	
	15	0.0561	4,859	11.82	1,5	*	
	16	0.00552	7,409	15.17	1,5	*	
	17	0.00187	9,513	11.68	1,5	*	
	18	0.00319	18,903	9.00	1,5	*	
	19	0.00146	8,568	12.87	1,5	*	
	20	0.00128	3,996	3.96	1,6	0	
	21	0.00132	7,568	14.73	1,5	*	
	22	0.000624	6,308	11.26	1,7	*	
	23	0.00102	4,184	4.81	0		
	24	0.00547	3,009	0.08	1,5	*	
	25	0.00125	3,243	50.24	1,4	+	
	26	0.00172	3,407	48.27	1,4	+	
	27	0.00157	5,109	47.84	1,4	+	
	28	0.00252	6,584	6.62	1,6	*	
	29	0.00732	5,598	9.60	1,5	*	
	30	0.00291	4,268	7.90	1,5	*	
	31	0.00422	4,017	9.45	1,5	*	
	32	0.00874	5,528	28.15	1,4	+	
	33	0.00179	3,009	21.13	1,4	*	

Table 4-10. Adjusted Data Results—Product 2 Only

Region	$1 - \alpha$	L	F	$n_1 n_2$	Significance Level	
1	0.000112	13,652	8.81	1,4	*	($\alpha = 0.05$)
2	0.000366	4,699	18.25	1,4	*	
3	0.000873	4,479	18.51	1,4	*	
4	0.000326	4,899	7.93	1,4	*	
5	0.000433	4,852	11.83	1,4	*	
6	0.000394	4,289	12.32	1,4	*	
7	0.000279	3,478	5.50	1,4	0	($\alpha = 0.10$)
8	0.000318	3,034	4.91	1,4	0	
9	0.000334	3,593	5.69	1,4	0	
10	0.000460	3,091	15.42	1,4	*	
11	0.000473	2,505	9.44	1,4	*	
12	0.000234	3,111	16.62	1,4	*	
13	0.000491	4,124	16.01	1,4	*	
14	0.000533	5,529	24.36	1,4	+	($\alpha = 0.01$)
15	0.000462	4,993	22.57	1,4	+	
16	0.000248	7,911	20.15	1,4	*	
17	0.000196	10,000	10.31	1,4	*	
18	0.000150	19,853	72.97	1,4	+	
19	0.000199	9,156	16.82	1,4	*	
20	0.000367	4,169	7.44	1,4	0	
21	0.000297	7,811	35.98	1,4	+	
22	0.000277	6,430	30.23	1,4	+	
23	0.000230	4,448	10.59	1,4	*	
24	0.000366	3,445	11.66	1,4	*	
25	0.000324	3,296	2.17	1,3		
26	0.000411	3,537	34.02	1,3	*	
27	0.000337	5,214	31.66	1,3	*	
28	0.0000841	6,516	2.02	1,4		
29	0.000254	6,008	11.22	1,4	*	
30	0.000355	4,597	9.07	1,4	*	
31	0.000951	4,224	54.58	1,4	+	
32	0.000874	5,528	28.15	1,4	+	
33	0.00179	3,009	21.13	1,4	*	

The value of $1 - \alpha$ is thought to be set quite early in the process of accepting the new product. Therefore, the measures of the effect of marketing actions on its value are drawn from the early marketing actions of the firm, where *early* is arbitrarily defined as the first two months of marketing action. We are now ready to define the measures precisely and predict their effect upon $1 - \alpha$.

First, remember that a higher value of $1 - \alpha$ implies a faster rate of approach to equilibrium. Therefore, $1 - \alpha$ should increase as the amount spent on promotions in the first two months (P_1) increases, as the amount spent on advertising in the first two months (A_1) increases, as the concurrent availability of the good (D_2) increases, and as the prior availability of the good (D_3) increases.[19]

The regression equation is

$$ADJ(1 - \alpha) \cdot 10^5$$

$$= 135.61 + 1.25D_3 + 0.0378P_1 - 0.244D_2 - 0.602A_1.$$

$$(0.233) \quad (0.252) \quad\quad (0.464) \quad\quad (0.510)$$

$F_{4,22} = 10.28$ (significant at $\alpha = 0.01$).

The results are not encouraging. Only promotions have the correct sign, and the coefficient for promotion effect is quite insignificant. Conversely, the coefficient for prior distribution is significant, but has a negative sign.[20] Probably the kindest thing that can be said about this result is that it leaves open the question of whether a firm's marketing strategy affects the rate at which consumers learn about a new product. It must also be kept in mind that no data were available for two other factors that might have an effect on the learning rate: consumer income and product price.

19. This corrects a comparative statics error I made in "A Theory of Consumer Behavior After Innovation."

20. If one could believe this, it would be a powerful argument against putting a product on the market without concurrent promotion and advertising.

Now we proceed to an investigation of the relation between L and the firm's marketing actions. Since L represents the asymptotic amount demanded in each region, it must first be divided by the population of the region N. When this is done, the dependent variable is L/N. We relate this variable to measures representing the firm's total marketing endeavor over the introductory period.

The variable L/N should increase as the per capita dollars spent on promotions, P, increase, as the per capita dollars spent on advertising, A, increase, as the final availability of the good, D, increases (i.e., the per cent of stores stocking the product at the end of the introductory period), and as the prior availability of the good, D_3, is greater. All these variables are based on the previously defined one-year introductory period. The result is

$$ADJ(L/N) = 0.543.97 + 5.31P + 0.747A + 0.789D_3 + 5.50D.$$
$$(2.07) \quad (1.44) \quad (2.54) \quad (10.2)$$

$F_{4,22} = 9.34$ (significant at $\alpha = .01$).

The coefficients all have the expected sign, but only that of promotions is significant. Dropping D_3, the least significant of the nonsignificant variables, the result becomes

$$ADJ(L/N) = -445.9 + 5.59P + 0.609A + 4.51D.$$
$$(1.84) \quad (1.34) \quad (9.53)$$

$F = 12.93$ (significant at $\alpha = .01$).

The results are basically the same.[21]

21. The corresponding regression from the unadjusted data is

$$L/N = 293.8 + 5.599P + 0.563A + 2.44D.$$
$$(1.90) \quad (1.39) \quad (9.87)$$
$$F = 11.44 \text{ (significant at } \alpha = 0.01).$$

The result is basically the same.

Thus it can be seen that the available empirical results do not reject, first, the basic theory, and, second, the idea that the effect of the firm's marketing actions can be summarized to a certain extent, at least for L/N, in terms of the effects of such marketing actions upon the parameters of the basic model.

However, in interpreting the results obtained in this section, it must be kept in mind that the estimates have been obtained by simple least-squares estimation in quite short time series. There is no assurance that the results obtained are, in a statistical sense, unbiased, efficient, or anything else. Further, single equations have clearly been extracted from what is possibly an interdependent economy. The difficulties inherent in these facts should be kept clearly in mind when the reported estimates are examined.

With this warning in mind, it is the author's opinion that the above results cannot be interpreted as denying the validity of the proposed theory. Because of the crudity and gaps in the data more than anything else, this is probably a fair summary of the meaning that one can safely attach to these results.

A Consideration of Possible Bias

The principle emphasis of the discussion to this point has been upon the specification of the basic model that assumes that the new product has no close technical substitutes or complements.[22] It seems sensible to address the possibility of testing this assumption. In the second part of Chapter 3, two different modifications of the model were discussed. It was shown that for the case of a new product that faces competition from a technical substitute, the resulting aggregate differential equation was

$$\frac{dY}{dn} = \lambda_2(1 - \alpha_2) + [\lambda_1(1 - \alpha_1) - \lambda_2(1 - \alpha_2) + \alpha_2 - 1]Y$$

$$- (\alpha_2 - \alpha_1)Y^2. \tag{3-19}$$

22. The two exceptions are the discussion of Carman's least-squares procedure and the briefly noted Kuehn, McGuire, and Weiss maximum-likelihood procedure.

Making the transformation to sales yields

$$\frac{1}{X}\frac{dX}{dt} = L_2(1 - \alpha_2)\frac{1}{X} + [L_1(1 - \alpha_1) - L_2(1 - \alpha_2) + \alpha_2 - 1]$$

$$-(\alpha_2 - \alpha_1)X \qquad (4\text{-}11)$$

The solution to this equation is quite complicated. That this is so may be readily seen from the result obtained by integrating by the methods used earlier for the simple model.

$$t = \frac{1}{\sqrt{b^2 - 4ac}} \ln \frac{2aX + b - \sqrt{b^2 - 4ac}}{2aX + b + \sqrt{b^2 - 4ac}}$$

where $a = -(\alpha_2 - \alpha_1)$
$b = L_1(1 - \alpha_1) - L_2(1 - \alpha_2) + \alpha_2 - 1$
$c = L_2(1 - \alpha_2)$.

The result, of course, has the form

$$X = K_1 + K_2\left(\frac{1 + K_3 e^{K_4 t}}{1 - K_3 e^{K_4 t}}\right)$$

where the K's are the appropriate functions of a, b, and c.

Once again the bias introduced by the assumption that (4-10) is correct when (4-11) actually is correct causes the rate of approach to equilibrium to appear higher than it actually is and to bias upward the estimated asymptote L_1. Thus the biasing effect of assuming (4-10) to be correct when it is not is quite clear in terms of the two alternative models presented here. This analysis should also clearly point out the need for care in interpreting the results presented earlier in this chapter.

The type of bias that equation (4-11) represents can be interpreted as arising from a situation in which another product on the market is a close technical substitute for the supposedly new product. It may be hypothesized that this would be the case for the second, third, fourth, and so on, brand of a new product put on the market, but not the first. The term $L_2(1 - \alpha_2)$ clearly represents the effect of the competing new product on the innovation.

Because (4-11) is different in form from the equation previously tested (4-7), it seemed interesting to rerun the previous set of data, using (4-11). This was done. Before the regressions were run, it was decided to set up the following criterion: If the added term is significant at $\alpha = 0.05$, using the standard F test for significance of an added variable to a regression, then the result should be interpreted as suggesting that bias could possibly be present in the previous estimates. It seemed possible that some bias might be found, because it was not clear that the company concerned was the first with the new product in all regions for which data existed. Table 4-11 presents the results.[22] Finally, it should be noted that although (4-11) can be used to test for bias, the parameters of the learning model in it are not identified, so that the equation cannot be used to estimate the underlying structural parameters.

By the previously stated criterion, 13 out of 33 regions show no evidence of bias. However, in four of these regions, 11, 23, 32, and 33, the sign of a_2 is correct, so perhaps bias exists in these that the statistical tests do not show.

It now seems sensible to turn to an examination of the simple hypothesis that the reason for bias is that the company concerned was not first on the market in the region with the new product. To do this, it is necessary to determine those regions in which the company was the first to market the new product type. Such data were available. Table 4-12 presents the results.

By treating this table as a 2×2 contingency table, a test may be readily made as to whether the two classifications are

22. A word of caution in interpreting these results is necessary. If dx/dt contains a random component, it will follow that $1/x$ will be positively correlated with $(1/x)(dx/dt)$ for spurious reasons. It is possible that some of the significance of the results of Table 4-11 may arise from this source.

Table 4-11. Bias Equation Estimates

$$R(t) = (1/X)(dX/dt) = a_0 + a_1 X + a_2 (1/X)$$

Region—Product 2	a_0	$-a_1$	a_2	$\hat{F}$	Does the Result Support Possible Bias
1	9.32	0.000662	−932	4.10	No
2	0.497	0.000208	2199	1216	Yes
3	180.4	0.0415	−137	1.76	No
4	0.126	0.000150	2898	10,813	Yes
5	0.903	0.000265	1876	2054	Yes
6	5.717	0.00127	−363	3.39	No
7	17.21	0.00537	−220	8.79	No
8	5.74	0.00211	−196	2.67	No
9	14.91	0.00438	−38.7	2.63	No
10	6.83	0.00221	−94.8	3.09	No
11	7.48	0.00313	45.1	23.88	No
12	0.597	−0.0000997	1065	19,903	Yes
13	0.883	0.000299	1427	1651	Yes
14	1.78	0.000384	1820	3904	Yes
15	0.942	0.000279	2186	1,151,000	Yes
16	0.605	0.000142	4032	27,060	Yes
17	0.731	0.000120	4407	2697	Yes
18	1.745	0.000104	6358	107,651	Yes
19	0.630	0.000113	3684	2310	Yes
20	6.54	0.00163	−309.8	1.68	No
21	1.22	0.000202	2695	1956	Yes
22	5.53	0.000885	−109.0	9.32	No
23	2.54	0.000602	85.7	3.05	No
24	0.0079	0.000112	1176	10,147	Yes
25	−0.891	0.0000177	3098	170.6	Yes
26	0.0314	0.000178	2104	3027	Yes
27	0.330	0.000189	3358	3891	Yes
28	3.54	0.000544	520.9	3978	Yes
29	0.303	0.000125	2599	27,175	Yes
30	0.562	0.000197	1534	1685	Yes
31	3.031	0.000751	71.55	2219	Yes
32	−0.163	0.0000868	4172	43.86	No
33	−0.0320	0.000203	2406	26.22	No

Table 4-12

	Product Is Not the First of Its Type	*Product Is the First of Its Type*
Bias	17	7
No Bias	4	5

independent.[23] The null hypothesis is that the probability that a region falls in any particular row is unaffected by the particular column to which it belongs. This means that rejection of the null hypothesis would suggest that the given simple theory of why bias arises is not obviously wrong.

Performing this test, one finds that

$$X_1{}^2 = 1.88 \not> \chi_1{}^2(@\alpha = 0.05) = 3.84$$

and that the null hypothesis cannot be rejected.

This result implies that the evidence does not support the simple theory that bias arises just because the product is not the first of its class in the market. It is, of course, easy to rationalize this result because the previously developed results suggest strongly that the marketing actions of competing firms would be very important also. Unfortunately, no data on marketing actions of competitive products were available, so this rationalization of the negative result cannot be subjected to test. This result, then, points to an area in which more work would be useful.

These findings demonstrate that not all the previous parameter estimates can be unreservedly accepted as being without bias. This does not necessarily mean, of course, that they are not useful. It has also been shown that care must be exercised in accepting the assumption that no substitutes exist. It has been demonstrated how to check the assumption of no substitutes.

23. For the mechanics of this test, see B. F. Ostle, *Statistics in Research*, Iowa State College Press, Ames, Iowa, 1954, pp. 138ff.

A tentative equation form to describe demand behavior when this assumption is wrong has been presented. Finally, these results point toward directions that may be taken in extending this work, particularly through relaxing the assumptions at the beginning of this paper.

Concluding Comments

This chapter has attempted to explicate the variety of possible methods of bringing the basic theory face to face with data. The inclusion of three appendices dealing with computational details should make it possible to replicate the basic results of this chapter and, given data, to proceed to further test the basic theory. The results in this chapter appear to support the theoretical notions so strongly that there can be no doubt that further empirical work is warranted.

Appendix B

Programs Relating to Carman Method

A Program for Market Analysis by Branching Tree

Gerald Waldstein

The Problem

This appendix presents a discussion of the construction of a branching-tree program to aid in the analysis of consumer panel data. It will be assumed that the consumer panel data have characteristics as follows. They are sorted and keyed on family identification numbers. The data for each family require four cards, one for each six-week period (there is a total of twenty-four weeks). Columns 1 through 12 give information about the family, including the area (seven geographical areas), family number, social class, age, children, household size, and whether or not they have television. Each week's data give whether or not there was a purchase (or any response at all) and if there was a purchase, the amount, brand, price, and store are given.

Given this mass of data, the problem is how to analyze it and, in particular, how to follow the pattern of buying for any brand we are interested in. For specificity, we shall assume interest in the new product—brand C, or brand 6 in the punch-card code.

The Algorithm

We now introduce the concept of a branching tree. Each week, we may ask the question, "Did the family purchase brand C?" The answer is "Yes" or "No." We can diagram this in the following manner. To take a point as the origin. (We shall call these points *nodes*.) It has two lines coming out of it to the right, one slanted up for "Yes" and one slanted down for "No." Each line ends in a node. So, if of ten families, six bought brand C the first week and four did not, we will have a tree with a node count as in Figure B-1.

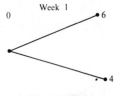

FIGURE B-1.

We may continue this analysis by asking, "Of the six who bought brand C the first week, how many bought it the second week?" and ask a similar question for the four who did not. We might get the results shown in Figure B-2.

In a similar manner, we can continue this indefinitely. However, since the number of nodes at each week is 2^n, we could not easily carry this out for the entire twenty-four weeks, because then the total number of nodes to consider would be

$$\sum_{i=1}^{24} 2^i.$$

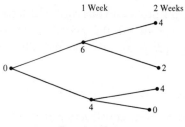

FIGURE B-2.

Instead, we decided to concentrate on six weeks of data, leaving only 126 (2 plus 4 plus 8 plus 16 plus 32 plus 64) nodes to study.

Here, a second question arose. Should a nonpurchase or a nonresponse be treated as the same as a purchase of a brand other than *C*? The answer is not intuitively clear; there are arguments to be considered for both sides. The problem was avoided by deciding to write a program that could consider either the first six *weeks* for each family or the first six *purchases* of a product.

Now we had two problems to attack: getting packed data and producing a tree. Also each family had certain demographic characteristics (social class, television, and so on). We wanted not only a node count but also a tally of the number of families possessing each attribute that went through a node. For example, for a given node, we would say six families passed through it. Of these, three were in class 1, two in class 2, one in class 4; five had television, one had not; and so on.

The Programs

There were two programs, the packing program, which read the data cards and punched a new card containing the family information and the block of information for each of the first six purchases. Thus, each group of four cards per family was condensed for our purposes into one card. The second, or branch-ing-tree program, produced the actual node and attributed counts. The second program is the theoretically more interesting one.

Branching-Tree Program

The main problem in constructing the tree is simply how to identify and number the nodes. We could number them con-secutively (Figure B-3).

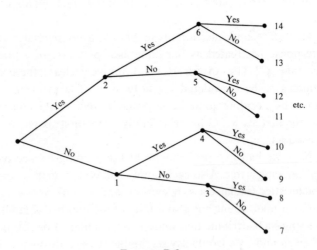

FIGURE B-3.

Now the problem is how to program the computer to read in the six numbers representing the six brands purchased and add 1 to the count of the six nodes making up the path for this family. An example seems to be called for.

Let us say that family 1003 (area 1, family 3) has bought, in the past six weeks brands 1, 3, 6, 6, 4, 7. Then, the path in the tree describing it would be as in Figure B-4 (we are interested in branch 6).

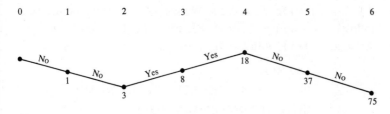

FIGURE B-4.

We want to add 1 to the count at each node it went through. Numbering them consecutively, as in the node-identification chart included at the end of this report, we can do this. But how to program it? There are two ways. The first is to use a list-processing system. Each node would be a list containing the name (address) of the node, the name of the node for "Yes" for the next week, the name of the node for "No" for the next week, and the count of families passing through the node. This, however, is clumsy and slow, as each card would cause several subroutines to occur.

The other way is to note that "Yes" and "No" correspond to binary numbers 0 and 1. A node can then be located by a string of 0's and 1's, corresponding to each week's "Yes" or "No" as to whether brand 6 was purchased. Thus, 1, 3, 6, 6, 4, 7 becomes 001100. The first node is identified as 0, the second as 00, the third as 001, the fourth as 0011, the fifth as 00110, and the sixth as 001100. Add 1 to the count at each node identified by each binary path, and the problem is solved.

However, a computer may not store binary numbers. I thought of converting to decimals, then using the decimal as a subscript. But 00 equals 000, i.e., the decimal equivalent for the node representing two weeks of nonpurchase equals the node for three weeks of nonpurchase and they are indistinguishable, so that this approach will not work.

Finally a solution was developed. We read in a string of six weeks' brand numbers, for example, 554663. Convert to 1's and

2's, rather than to 0's and 1's. We get 111221. Then we use the following Fortran loop (from left to right, the numbers in the string are $NDAT_i$ with $i = 1, \ldots, 6$):

$$DO\ 50\ JI = 1, 6$$
$$NUMB = NDAT(JI)*(2**(JI-1)) + NUMB$$
$$SUM(NUMB) = SUM(NUMB) + 1.0$$

This creates a decimal equivalent for the first number, then the first two numbers, the first three numbers, and so on. In our example, the computer would go like this (NUMB is zeroed at initialization of each read-in):

$$JI = 1, \text{ so } NUMB = 1*2^0*0 = 1$$
$$\text{then } SUM(1) = SUM(1) + 1.0 \leftarrow \text{Floating}$$
$$\text{sum} = \text{node count}$$
$$JI = 2, \text{ so } NUMB = 1*2^1 + 1 = 3$$
$$SUM(3) = SUM(3) + 1.0$$

and so on, with SUM(NUMB) being the node count. Counts are also done for attributes by using double subscripts, one for the node, the other for the attribute classification. (See Figure B-6.) This results in the node-numbering system shown in Figure B-5. All nodes in the lower half of the tree are odd numbered, and in the upper half are even numbered. The key number in the system is 2^{i-1}, where i is the purchase number.

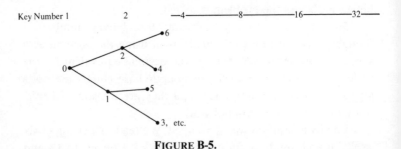

FIGURE B-5.

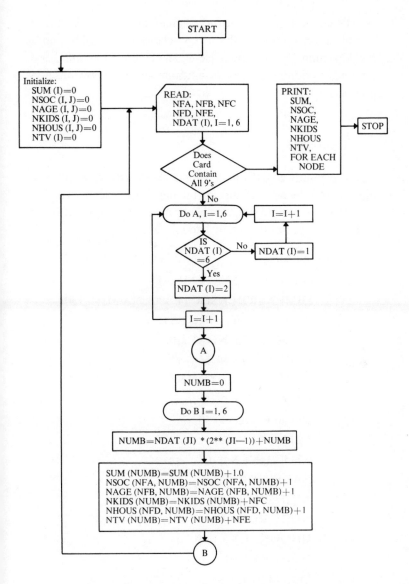

FIGURE B-6. Branching Tree Program Flow Chart.

From each node, the corresponding non-purchase-node identification number for the next purchase is obtained by adding the key number; the purchase-node identification number is obtained by adding 2 times the key number to the previous node number.

The Results

The results give the node counts for the entire sample, then break down the node counts for the number in each social class, age group, household size, whether or not the family had children, and whether or not the family had television.

Program Listing

ST NO FORTRAN STATEMENT

```
      DIMENSION NSOC (4, 130), NAGE (4, 130),
        NKIDS (130), NHOUS (5, 130)
      DIMENSION NDAT (10)
      DIMENSION SUM (130)
      DIMENSION NTV (130)
      DO 41 L = 1,4
      DO 40 KKK = 1,130
      SUM(KKK) = 0.0
      NSOC(L,KKK) = 0
      NAGE(L,KKK) = 0
      NKIDS(KKK) = 0
      NHOUS(L,KKK) = 0
      NHOUS(5,KKK) = 0
      NTV(KKK) = 0
   40 CONTINUE
   41 CONTINUE
```

```
   5    FORMAT(7X,511,2X,6(4X,I1,6X))
 100    READ 5,NFA,NFB,NFC,NFD,NFE,(NDAT(I),
           I = 1,6)
        IF (NDAT(1) − 9)6,500,500
   6    DO 9 I = 1,6
        IF(NDAT(I) − 6)7,8,7
   7    NDAT(I) = 1
        GO TO 9
   8    NDAT(I) = 2
   9    CONTINUE
  15    NUMB = 0
        DO 50 JI = 1,6
        NUMB = NDAT(JI)*(2**(JI − 1)) + NUMB
        SUM(NUMB) = SUM(NUMB) + 1.0
        NSOC(NFA,NUMB) = NSOC(NFA,NUMB) + 1
        NAGE(NFB,NUMB) = NAGE(NFB,NUMB) + 1
        NKIDS(NUMB) = NKIDS(NUMB) + NFC
        NHOUS(NFD,NUMB) = NHOUS(NFD,NUMB)
           + 1
        NTV(NUMB) = NTV(NUMB) + NFE
  50    CONTINUE
        GO TO 100
 500    DO 510 I = 1,130
        IF(SUM(I)) 510,510,501
 501    PRINT 502,I,SUM(I)
 502    FORMAT (4HNODE,I5,4X,6HCOUNTS,F6.0)
 505    DO 509 LK = 1,4
        PRINT 506,I,NSOC(LK,I),LK
 506    FORMAT (4HNODE,I5,5X,I5,2X,I3HWERE IN
           CLASS,I3)
```

```
509    CONTINUE
       DO 540 LK = 1,4
       PRINT 512,I,NAGE(LK,I),LK
512    FORMAT (4HNODE,I5,5X,I5,2X,17HWERE IN
          AGE GROUP,I3)
540    CONTINUE
       DO 54I LK = 1,5
       PRINT 513,I,NHOUS(LK,I),LK
513    FORMAT (4HNODE,I5,5X,I5,2X,21HHAD
          HOUSEHOLD SIZE OF,I3)
541    CONTINUE
       NSM = SUM(I)
       NID = NSUM - NKIDS(I)
       NOV = NSUM - NTV(I)
521    FORMAT (4HNODE,I5,5X,I5,2X,16HHAD
          CHILDREN, ANDI5,2X,8HHAD NONE)
522    FORMAT (4HNODE,I5,5X,I5,2X,10HHAD TV,
          AND15,2X,5HHADNT)
       PRINT 521,I,NKIDS(I),NID
       PRINT 522,I,NTV(I),NOV
510    CONTINUE
 99    STOP
       END
```

A Program for Carman's Estimation Procedure

R. L. Baumann

Program to Compute Parameters β, $\pounds_P$, $\pounds_R$

Variable Dictionary

YPBAR	$\overline{Y}_P$
YRBAR	$\overline{Y}_R$
XBAR	$\overline{X}$
ALFAP	α_P
ALFAR	5_R
SUM1	$\Sigma Y_P X$
SUM2	$\Sigma Y_R X$
SUMX	ΣX
SUMX2	ΣX^2
SUMYP	ΣY_P
SUMYR	ΣY_R
TRIP	N
BHAT	$\hat{\beta}$

Program Listing

```
C       PROGRAM TO COMPUTE PARAMETERS
            B,ALFAP,ALFAR
C       RLBAUMANN
        SUM1 = 0.0
        SUM2 = 0.0
        SUMX = 0.0
        SUMX2 = 0.0
        SUMYP = 0.0
        SUMYR = 0.0
```

```
        TRIP = 0.0
   1    READ 5,X,YSUBP,YSUBR
   5    FORMAT (3F10.4)
        IF(X)10,10,2
   2    SUM1 = SUM1 + YSUBP*X
        SUM2 = SUM2 + X**2
        SUMYR = SUMYR + YSUBR
        SUMYP = SUMYP + YSUBP
        TRIP = TRIP + 1.0
        GO TO 1
  10    SI1 = (TRIP*(SUM1 + SUM2) - SUMX*
           (SUMYR + SUMYP))
        SI2 = (2.0*TRIP*SUMX2)
        SI3 = (2.0*(SUMX**2))
        BHAT = SI1/(SI2 - SI3)
        YPBAR = SUMYP/TRIP
        XBAR = SUMX/TRIP
        ALFAP = YPBAR - (BHAT*XBAR)
        YRBAR = SUMYR/TRIP
        ALFAR = YRBAR - (BHAT*XBAR)
        PUNCH 5,BHAT,ALFAP,ALFAR
        PRINT 5,BHAT,ALFAP,ALFAR
        PUNCH 5,XBAR,YPBAR,YRBAR
        PRINT 5,XBAR,YPBAR,YRBAR
        STOP
        END
```

Program to Compute R^2 and t for Results of Previous Program

Variable Dictionary

B	β
AP	α_P
AR	α_R
XN	N
XBAR	$\overline{X}$
YPBAR	$\overline{Y}_P$
YRBAR	$\overline{Y}_R$
YP	Y_P
YR	Y_{R_2}
RSQ	R
DF	Degrees of freedom
UVYP	Unassociated variation in Y_P
UVYR	Unassociated variation in Y_R
TVYP	Total variation in Y_P
TVYR	Total variation in Y_R

Program Listing

```
C         PROGRAM TO COMPUTE R2 AND T
C         RLBAUMANN
          UVYP=0
          UYYR=0
          TVYP=0
          TVYR=0
          XN=0
          READ 5,B,AP,AR
          READ 5,XBAR,YPBAR,YRBAR
     1    READ 5,X,YP,YR
     5    FORMAT (3F10.4)
```

```
        IF(X)10,10,2
   2    UVYP = UVYP + (YP − AP − B*X)**2
        UVYR = UVYR + (YR − AR − B*X)**2
        TVYP = TVYP + (YP − YPBAR)**2
        TVYR = TVYR + (YR − YRBAR)**2
        XN = XN + 1.0
        GO TO 1
  10    RSQ = 1.0 − ((UVYR + UVYP)/(TVYR + TVYP))
        R = SQRTF (RSQ)
        DF = XN − 2.0
        T = (R*SQRTF(DF))/(SQRTF(1.0 − RSQ))
        PUNCH 5,RSQ,DF,T
        STOP
        END
```

Appendix C

Computer Programs for Minimum χ^2 Parameter Estimation

Gary L. Grahn

Program to Compute Parameter Estimates Assuming Constant Weights

Variable Dictionary

I	Subscript over trials (v)
AN(I)	Number of families buying in week I
TFAM	Total number of families (constant)
AP(I)	$\hat{p}$, estimate of p for the Ith week; if no families or one family purchased then $\hat{p} = 0$ by convention
OMEGA	Maximum number of trials
SUMPH	Sum of the $\hat{p}$'s
SUMPA	Sum of the $\hat{p}$'s multiplied by the ALPHA(J)
A	One increment (value of XINC) less than XSTRT (starting value)
ALMAX	Maximum number of alpha values desired

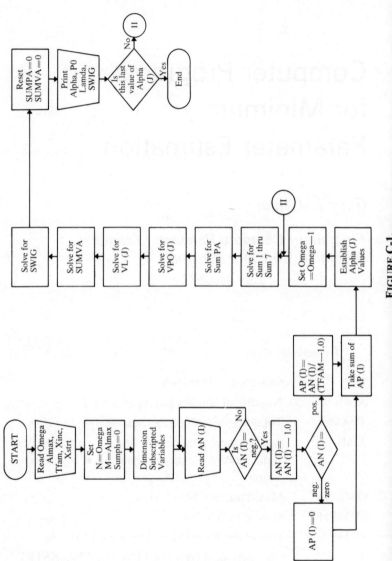

FIGURE C-1.

ALPHA(J)	Value between 0 and 1, whose range is predetermined
VPO(J)	P_0
VL(J)	$\lambda(J)$
SWIG(J)	Figure used as dummy which should approximate zero

Computer Program Listings

```
C          VARIABLE DICTIONARY
C          I = SUBSCRIPT OVER TRIALS(V)
C          AN(I)=NUMBER OF FAMILIES BUYING IN
               WEEK I
C          TFAM=TOTAL NUMBER OF FAMILIES
               (CONSTANT)
C          AP(I)= P HAT
C          OMEGA = MAXIMUM NUMBER OF TRIALS
               (CONSTANT)
C          SUMPH = SUM OF THE P HATS
C          SUMPA = SUM OF THE P HATS
               MULTIPLIED BY THE ALPHA (J)
C          A = ONE INCREMENT (VALUE OF XINC)
               LESS THAN XSTRT (STARTING VALUE)
C          ALMAX = MAXIMUM NUMBER OF ALPHA
               VALUES DESIRED
C          BEGIN PROGRAM
C          FOR GENERALIZED PROGRAM DO THE
               FOLLOWING
           READ 2,OMEGA,ALMAX,TFAM,XINC,XSTRT
     2     FORMAT (1X,3F8.0,2F7.5)
```

```
C              1ST DATA CARD MUST HAVE OMEGA VAL
                  IN COL 2–9, ALMAX VAL IN 10–17, TFAM
C       1      VAL IN 18–25, XUNC in 26–32, XSTRT IN 33–39,
                  ALL IN FLOATING POINT
               N = OMEGA
               M = ALMAX
               DIMENSION AP(30),AN(30),ALPHA(30),
                  VPO(30),VL(30),SWIG(30)
               SUMPA = 0.0
               SUMVA = 0.0
        1      FORMAT (1X,24F3.0)
               DO 125 I – 1,N
               READ 3,AP(I)
C              AP(I) INPUTS, 1 TO A CARD, V VALUE (NOT
                  READ) IN COL 1–3, AP(I) IN 4–9 FP
      125      CONTINUE
C              PORTION TO COMPUTE SUM P HAT
               SUMPH – 0.0
               DO 200 I = 1,N
               SUMPH – SUMPH + AP(I)
      200      CONTINUE
               DO 205 I = 1,N
               PRINT 201,AP(I)
      201      FORMAT (8F10.8)
      205      CONTINUE
C              PORTION TO ESTABLISH ALPHA VALUES
               A = XSTRT – XINC
               DO 250 J – 1,M
               A = A + XINC
               ALPHA(J) = A
```

```
  250     CONTINUE
          OMEGA = OMEGA - 1.0
C         NOW START SUM 1 TO SUM 7
             COMPUTATIONS
          DO 300 J = 1,M
          ASUM = 1.0 - (ALPHA(J)**(OMEGA + 1.0))
          BSUM - 1.0 - ALPHA(J)
          SUM1 = ASUM/BSUM
          CSUM = ALPHA(J)**((2.0*OMEGA) + 2.0)
          XSUM = 1.0 - (ALPHA(J)**2.0)
          SUM2 = (1.0 - CSUM)/XSUM
          DSUM = (BSUM)*(OMEGA + 1.0)*
             (ALPHA(J)**OMEGA)
             SUM3 = (ASUM - DSUM)/(BSUM**2.0)
          ESUM = ALPHA(J)*(1.0 - CSUM)
          FSUM = XSUM*(OMEGA + 1.0)*
             (ALPHA(J)**((2.0*OMEGA) + 1.0))
          GSUM = XSUM**2.0
          SUM4 = (ESUM - FSUM)/GSUM
          SUM5 = OMEGA + 1.0 - SUM1
          SUM6 = SUM1 - SUM2
          SUM7 = SUM3 - SUM4
          PRINT 10,SUM1,SUM2,SUM3,SUM4,SUM5,
             SUM6,SUM7
   10     FORMAT (1X,7E11.5)
C         REMOVE AFTER DEBUGGING
C         NESTED DO LOOP NEEDED FOR
             CALCULATIONS
          DO 275 I = 1,N
          C = I - 1
```

```
              SUMPA = SUMPA + (AP(I)*(ALPHA(J)**C))
        275   CONTINUE
              PRINT 10,SUMPH,ASUM,BSUM,CSUM,DSUM,
                 XSUM,SUMPA
   C          CALCULATION OF THE P(0) AND LAMBDA
                 VALUES
              VPO(J) = ((SUMPH*SUM6) −
                 (SUMPA*SUM5))/((SUM1*SUM6) −
                 (SUM2*SUM5))
              VL(J) = (SUMPH − (VPO(J)*SUM1))/SUM5
   C          NESTED DO LOOP FOR THE CALCULATION
                 OF SWIG
              DO 285 K = 1,N
              B = K − 1
              SUMVA = SUMVA + ((B)*(ALPHA(J)**(B − 1.0))*
                 AP(K))
              SWIG(J) = (VPO(J)*SUM4) + (VL(J)*SUM7) =
                 SUMVA
        285   CONTINUE
              PRINT 15,ALPHA(J),VPO(J),VL(J),SWIG(J)
              SUMPA = 0.0
              SUMVA = 0.0
         15   FORMAT (1X,10HALPHA IS ,F7.5/1X,8H PO
                 IS ,F10.5/1X,12H LAMBDA IS
          1      ,F10.5/1X,10H SWIG IS ,F10.5)
        300   CONTINUE
              STOP
```

Program to Establish "Best" Alpha Value

Variable Dictionary

I	Subscript over trials (v)
AN(I)	Number of families buying in week I
AP(I)	$\hat{p}$, unbiased estimate of $PV(I)$
OMEGA	Maximum number of trials
VP(I)	Probability of purchase
W(I)	Weight associated with trial I
VPO	P_0
ALPH1	α_1 value
VL1	λ_1 value
VL1A	Intermediate value of λ_1
VL1B	Intermediate value of λ_1
SWIG	Figure used as dummy which should approximate zero

Logic

1. Input the previous $X_v, P_0, \alpha_1, \lambda, \Omega$
2. Compute $p(v)$'s, using

$$p(v) = \alpha_1{}^v p_0 + (1 + \alpha_1{}^v)\lambda_1,$$

which gives a new set of $p(v)$'s.

3. Compute weights using

$$W_v = \frac{X_v}{p_v{}^2(1 - p_v)}.$$

4. Using equations 10-40, 10-41, 10-42, go through a direct search routine to find values of P_0, α, λ, which minimize SWIG.

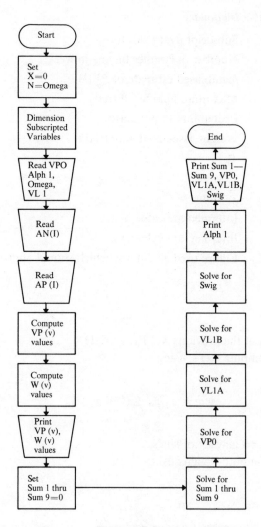

FIGURE C-2.

(Equations are from Bush and Mosteller, *op. cit.*, p. 231.)

$$P_0 \sum_v W_v \alpha_1{}^v + \lambda_1 \sum_v W_V(1 - \alpha_1{}^v) = \sum_v W_v \hat{P}_v \quad (\textbf{10-40})$$

$$P_0 \sum_v W_v \alpha_1{}^{2v} + \lambda_1 \sum_v W_v \alpha_1{}^v(1 - \alpha_1{}^v) = \sum_v W_v{}^V \hat{P}_0 \alpha_1 V \quad (\textbf{10-41})$$

$$\xi(\alpha_1) = P_0 \sum_v W_v V \alpha_1{}^{2v-1} + \lambda_1 \sum_v W_v V \alpha_1{}^{v-1}(1 - \alpha_1{}^v)$$

$$- \sum_v W_v v \alpha_1{}^v + \hat{P}_v + 0 \quad (\textbf{10-42})$$

Program Listing

```
*JOB KC011 GRAHN
*XEQ
*DUMP
*FORMAT N
*LIST
*FAP
C         VARIABLE DICTIONARY
C         I = SUBSCRIPT OVER TRIALS(V)
C         AN(I) = NUMBER OF FAMILIES BUYING IN
              WEEK I
C         AP(I) = P HAT
C         OMEGA = MAXIMUM NUMBER OF TRIALS
              (CONSTANT)
          DIMENSION AP(30),AN(30),VP(30),W(30)
          X = 0.0
          READ 6,VPO,ALPH1,VL1,OMEGA
          N = OMEGA
          DO 150 I = 1,N
          READ 5,AN(I)
```

```
      105   CONTINUE
            DO 106 I = 1,N
            READ 7,AP(I)
      106   CONTINUE
        4   FORMAT (1X,45HFOLLOWING RESULTS
                WERE OBTAINED WITH   = ,F10.5/
                141X,5HPO =  ,F10.5/37X,9HLAMBDA =
                ,F10.5)
        5   FORMAT (9X,F6.4)
        7   FORMAT (9X,F10.7)
       10   PUNCH 4,APLH1,VPO,VL1
C             START TO COMPUTE P(V) VALUES
            DO 20 J = 1,N
            V = J − 1
            VP(J) = ((ALPH1**V)*VPO) +
                ((1.0 − (ALPH1**V))*VL1)
C             START TO COMPUTE W(V) VALUES
            W(J) − (AN(J))/((VP(J)**2.0)*(1.0 − VP(J)))
            PUNCH 8,J,VP(J),J,W(J)
        8   FORMAT (fX,2HP( ,I2,6H) IS , F10.5,5X2HW
                ( ,I2,6H) IS ,F10.2)
       20   CONTINUE
       21   CONTINUE
            SUM1 = 0.0
            SUM2 = 0.0
            SUM3 = 0.0
            SUM4 = 0.0
            SUM5 = 0.0
            SUM6 = 0.0
            SUM7 = 0.0
```

```
        SUM8 = 0.0
        SUM9 = 0.0
        M = OMEGA
        DO 22 K = 1,M
        V = K - 1
        SUM1 = SUM1 + (W(K)*(ALPH1**V))
        SUM2 = SUM2 + (W(K)*(1.0 - (ALPH1**V)))
        SUM3 = SUM3 + (W(K)*AP(K))
        SUM4 = SUM4 + (W(K)*((ALPH1)**(2.0*V)))
        SUM5 = SUM5 + (W(K)*(ALPH1**V)*
           (1.0 - (ALPH1**V)))
        SUM6 = SUM6 + (W(K)*AP(K)*(ALPH1**V))
        SUM7 = SUM7 + (W(K)*V*(ALPH1**
           (2.0*V - 1.0)))
        SUM8 = SUM8 + (W(K)*V*(ALPH1**(V - 1.0))*
           (1.0 - (ALPH1**V)))
        SUM9 = SUM9 + (W(K)*V*(ALPH1**(V - 1.0))*
           AP(K))
    22  CONTINUE
C       PORTION TO COMPUTE NEW VALUES OF
           VPO,VL1,SWIG
        VPO - (SUM3*SUM5 - SUM6*SUM2)/
           (SUM1*SUM5 - SUM4*SUM2)
        VL1a - (SUM3 - (VPO*SUM1))/SUM2
        VL1B = (SUM6 - (VPO*SUM4))/SUM5
           SWIG - VPO*SUM7 + VL1A*SUM8 - SUM9
        PUNCH 24,ALPH1
        PUNCH 25,SUM1,SUM2,SUM3,SUM4,SUM5,
           SUM6,SUM7,SUM8,SUM9,VPO,VL1A,1VL1B,
           SWIG
```

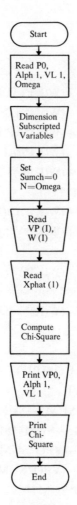

FIGURE C-3.

```
24    FORMAT (/1X,45HFOLLOWING RESULTS
      WERE OBTAINED WITH ALPH1= ,F10.5)
25    FORMAT (1X,9HSUM1 IS ,E12.4/1X,9HSUM2 IS
      E12.4/1X,9HSUMB IS ,1E12.4/1X,9HSUM4 is
      ,E12.4/1X,9HSUM5 is , 2.4/1X,9HSUM6 is ,
      2E12.4/1X,9HSUM7 IS ,E12.4/1X,9HSUM8 IS ,
      2.4/1X,9HSUM9 IS , 3E12.4/1X,7HPO IS
      ,F10.5/1X,12HLAMBDAA IS F10.5/1X,
      12HLAMBDAB I 4S ,F10.5/1X,9HSWIG is
      ,F10.2)
      VL1 = VL1A
30    CONTINUE
```

Program to Compute χ^2

Variable Dictionary

I	Subscript over trials (v)
W(I)	Weight associated with trial I
VP(I)	Probability of purchase
XPHAT(I)	Estimate of VP for the Ith week
OMEGA	Maximum number of trials
VPO	P_0 value determined from previous program
ALPH1	Value of α_1 determined from previous program
VL1	Value of λ_1 determined from previous program

Program Listing

```
*JOB KC     GRAHN
*XEQ
*DUMP
*FORMAT N
```

```
*LIST
*EAP
C       PROGRAM TO COMPUTE CHI SQUARE
        DIMENSION W(24),VP(24),XPHAT(24)
   2    FORMAT (10X,F12.5,13X,F12.2)
   3    FORMAT (///13HCHI SQUARE = ,F12.5///)
   4    FORMAT (1X,45HFOLLOWING RESULTS
          WERE OBTAINED WITH ALPH1 = ,F10.5/
          141X,5HPO= ,F10.5/37X,9HLAMBDA =
          ,F10.5)
   6    FORMAT (1X,F10.5,F7.5,F7.5,F8.0)
   7    FORMAT (10X,F8.5)
   8    FORMAT (1X,2HP(.12.6H) IS ,F10.5,5X2HW
          (.12.6H) IS .F10.2.5X,3HPH
        1( ,12,6H) IS ,F10.5)
        READ 6,VPO,ALPH1,VL1,OMEGA
        SUMCH=0.0
        N=OMEGA
        DO55I=1,N
        READ 7,XPHAT(I)
  55    CONTINUE
        DO 9 I=1,N
        READ 2,VP(I),W(I)
        DO 10 I=1,N
          X=W(I)*((VP(I)-XPHAT(I))*
            (VP(I)-XPHAT(I)))
          SUMCH=SUMCH+X
     10   CONTINUE
        PRINT 4,ALPH1,VPO,VL1
        PRINT 3, SUMCH
```

```
          DO 15 J = 1,N
          PRINT 8,J,VP(J),J,W(J),J,XPHAT(J)
    15    CONTINUE
          STOP
          END
*DATA
0.0038    0.319 0.0065 24.0
          0.00387
          0.00290
          0.00484
          0.00484
          0.00096
          0.00387
          0.00096
          0.00193
          0.00096
          0.00484
          0.00290
ZZJOB   KC011 GRAHN
ZZFORX53
C         PROGRAM TO COMPUTE CHI SQUARES
              FROM TEXT DATA
          DIMENSION AP(30)
    3     FORMAT (3X,F20.5)
    4     FORMAT (F5.0,4F10.5)
    5     FORMAT (F15.10)
    6     FORMAT (F5.0,3F10.5)
          READ 6,OMEGA,XPHAT,ALPHA,XLAMB
          SUMCH = 0.0
          N = OMEGA
```

```
         DO 125 I = 1,N
         READ 3,AP(I)
C        AP(I) INPUTS, 1 TO A CARD, V VALUF(NOT
            READ) IN COL 1-3,AP(I)
         IN 4-9FP
   125   CONTINUE
         DO 15 I = 1,N
         C = I - 1
         X = (((ALPHA**C)*XPHAT) + ((1.0 - (ALPHA**C))
            *XLAMB) - AP(I))**2.0
         PRINT 5,X
         SUMCH = SUMCH + X
    15   CONTINUE
```

Likelihood Function Evaluation Program

Variable Dictionary

ALOGL	$\ln \mathscr{L}$
ALV	$\alpha_1{}^V$
AL1	α_1
ANV	N_V
BL1	λ_1
I	i
N	Ω
PO	P_0
V	v
X	X_v
Z1	
Z2	
Z3	Intermediate working variables
Z4	
Z5	

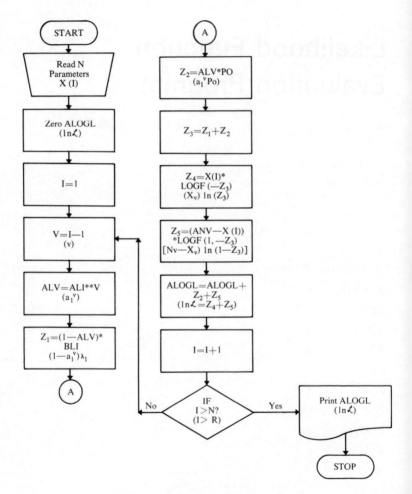

FIGURE D-1. Flow Diagram.

Program Listing

```
      PROGRAM TO EVALUATE LIKELIHOOD
        FUNCTION
      DIMENSION X(24(
      READ 1,N,ANV,PO,AL1,BL1
  1   FORMAT (I2,F4.0,3F7.5)
      READ 2,X
  2   FORMAT (24F2.0)
 10   ALOGL=0
      I=1
  3   V=I−1
      ALV=ALI**V
      Z1=(1.−ALV)*BL1
      Z2=ALV*PO
      Z3=Z1+Z2
      Z4=X(I)*LOGF(Z3)
      Z5=(ANV−X(I))*LOGF(1.−Z3)
      ALOGL=ALOGL+Z4+Z5
      I=I+1
      IF(I−N) 4, 4, 5
  4   GO TO 3
  5   PRINT 6,ALOGL
  6   FORMAT (1X,GHANSWER/1X,GHLOG
        L=F12.6)
      READ 1,N,ANV,PO,AL1,BL1
      IF(N) 1 1, 1 1, 1 0
 11   CONTINUE
      STOP
      END
```

*DATA
2410330.037600.325   0.00362
5 4 6 6 2 5 2 3 2 6 4 4 2 8 2 6 4 1 4 8 8 7 8 7
2410330.003630.319   0.00654
2410330.003600.319   0.00654
2410330.003690.319   0.00654
2410330.003630.320   0.00654
2410330.003630.318   0.00654
2410330.003630.319   0.00659
2410330.003630.319   0.00650
2410330.003800.315   0.00650
00
N ANX PO α_1 λ_1

Chapter 5

Extensions and Applications

The preceding discussion of the general theoretical framework and its use in data analysis has raised a set of issues on which discussion was deferred to enable an orderly presentation of the central concepts. This chapter will provide a discussion of these topics. First the application of the model to durable goods will be discussed, then the issue of measuring product preferences. The third section discusses the relation between the model considered and two alternate models of consumer behavior. Finally, the chapter and book end with a few brief concluding comments.

Durable Goods

The central aspect of handling new durable goods within the framework of the previously defined model arises from a basic difference in the conception of how consumers behave during the shopping and learning process. Udell has shown that the shopping behavior of consumers is different for durables than for nondurables.[1] The nature of this difference is as follows. Shopping for nondurables, the consumer gains information by purchasing and trying out the product in use. In the case of durables, such a process would be costly indeed. Therefore the consumer typically engages in extensive search behavior prior to purchasing any durable good.

This extensive search behavior means that an individual consumer learns about the characteristics of the product during the shopping process, not during the processes of repetitive use of products as is the case when nondurable products are involved. The implication is that it is not possible to verify the basic underlying theory by observation of individual behavior without resorting to methods similar to those discussed by Robert King in Appendix A. However, the aggregate characteristics of behavior can be tested once the consequences of the difference in shopping behavior are understood: namely, that the appropriate aggregate measure is the stock of the durable in use by consumers or the probability of owning a particular durable. Given the difference in shopping behavior, this fact is quite apparent.

This is a very simple matter once it has been stated. It is also of substantial importance in a practical sense, because there are several empirical studies of the increase in use of new durable goods that tend to provide support for this deduction from the underlying theory.

For example, Mansfield's study of the spread of technological innovation in an industry may be interpreted as giving empirical support.[2] The basic equation is that derived in Chapter 3.

1. John G. Udell, "Prepurchase Behavior of Buyers of Small Electrical Appliances," *Journal of Marketing*, vol. 30, no. 4, October, 1966.
2. E. Mansfield, "Technological Change and the Rate of Imitation," *Econometrica*, vol. 29, no. 4, October, 1961.

$$Y = \frac{\lambda}{1 - \exp\left[-a_1 - (1 - \alpha_1)\lambda n\right]} \qquad (3\text{-}17)$$

Assume that trials can be roughly approximated by time since trials are not directly observable. Hence,

$$Y_t = \frac{\lambda}{1 - \exp\left[-a_1 - (1 - \alpha_1)\lambda t\right]}. \qquad (5\text{-}1)$$

In some applications, λ is fixed or known. Concurrently with this, a maximum number of responses N can be defined in some of these situations. Although it is difficult to imagine these conditions being met in the case of consumer nondurable goods, in a case such as the spread of technological innovation among the firms in an industry these conditions are quite reasonable. In this situation, the number of firms is given by definition, and it is often sensible to assume that all firms in the industry will eventually adopt the innovation. Thus the maximum number of responses is given, and both sides of (5-1) can be multiplied by this to yield

$$M_t = \frac{N\lambda}{1 - \exp\left[-a_1 - (1 - \alpha_1)\lambda t\right]}. \qquad (5\text{-}2)$$

If $\lambda = 1$ (i.e., all firms in the industry are assumed to adopt the innovation eventually), then

$$M_t = \frac{N}{1 - \exp\left[-a_1 - (1 - \alpha_1)\lambda t\right]}. \qquad (5\text{-}3)$$

Equation (5-3) is the equation form Mansfield used to study the spread of technological innovations in an industry. He reports that this equation "represents the data for most of the innovations [studied] quite well."[3] He also studied factors that affect the rate of organizational learning; the results tend to support

3. *Ibid.*, p. 751.

the notion that the learning rate is higher for more profitable innovations and for ones requiring a small capital investment.[4]

A similar model is found in the pioneering work of Joseph Yance.[5] Yance deals with the increase in use of diesels by the railroad industry. He argues, basically, that (1) it is not necessary to build a model motivated by learning behavior in order to understand the process of investment in a technological innovation by an industry, and (2) that the experience of the industry with innovation is crucially important in the accepting process. This is, of course, quite similar to the argument presented for consumer nondurables.

He then develops an epidemiological model that is not directly testable. Next, he tests a difference-equation approximation to (3-16), where the variables have been transformed from probabilities to diesel stock in raw numbers of diesels. Yance argues that this equation approximates the epidemiological model, which in turn captures some important elements of points 1 and 2. In fact, as has been shown, this equation is a direct implication of points 1 and 2, given the assumptions presented in Chapter 3.

The empirical result is

$$\Delta K_t = 0.0000016598 K_{t-1}(27{,}300 - K_{t-1})$$

$$r = 0.98$$

$$K_t = \text{stock of diesel units in year } t.$$

4. It should be noted that the derivation of the logistic presented by Mansfield differs from that presented here in that he uses a diffusion-type derivation. There is no inconsistency between the two derivations; however, the parameters of the resulting logistic do have slightly different interpretations. In the learning derivation, these parameters must be taken as affected by interpersonal learning; in the diffusion derivation, the parameters are presumed to be affected by individual learning. It can be readily seen, therefore, that with such aggregate data it is not possible to separate the effects of individual learning from learning induced by interpersonal interaction.

5. J. V. Yance, "Investment Behavior in the Railroad Industry," Harvard University, Cambridge, Massachusetts: Ph.D. thesis, 1955. See also his later unpublished paper, "Technological Change as a Learning Process," no date.

This empirical result of Yance's is really somewhat surprising, because one of the basic assumptions required for the logistic to be theoretically correct is the each user purchase only one of the new durables during the introductory period. This assumption is clearly incorrect. In fact, if we assume that a firm engages in learning behavior during the process of introducing new durables, then the number or proportion of the new durable units in use ought to be logistic. Mansfield has tested this hypothesis for diesel locomotives and finds it is not rejected.[6]

Therefore, the basic theory predicts for durable goods a logistic equation for both number of firms and number of units per firm over time. The aggregate is therefore a sum of a number of logistic equations, each starting at a different time. It is well known that in such a case the aggregate equation has the form

$$y = \frac{K}{1 + m \exp\left[a_1 t + a_2 t^2 + \cdots + a_n t^n\right]}$$

where $n > 1$, $a_n < 0$, and n is odd.[7] In this case, a logistic is a first approximation to the theoretically correct equation. Yance's results seem to indicate that the first approximation may be a very good one, but there is no a priori reason to expect this in all cases.

Griliches uses (5-2) in his study of the increase in the use of hybrid corn.[8] The Griliches article illustrates an important point. It is that in (5-2) λ appears on both the top and the bottom on the right-hand side. It is clearly possible to confuse factors that affect the limit with those affecting the rate of learning. Griliches is careful to separate the two effects. He finds, for instance, that a semisociological variable, importance of corn to the farmer, affects $\lambda(0_k)$ but not $f(z_j)$.

6. E. Mansfield, "Intrafirm Rates of Diffusion of an Innovation," *The Review of Economics and Statistics*, vol. 45, no. 4, November, 1963, pp. 348–359.

7. The original proof is given in H. S. Pearl and L. J. Reed, "On the Mathematical Theory of Population Growth," *Metron*, vol. 3, no. 1, 1923, pp. 6ff.

8. Z. Griliches, "Hybrid Corn," *Econometrica*, vol. 25, no. 4, October, 1957.

In regard to this, it is useful to stop and note the results of the work of rural sociologists on the diffusion of innovation.

Rural sociologists have generally worked in this area with what appear to be linear models.[9] However, the data represent scaled data and so may be scaled to actually represent a logarithmic-type transform often used in estimating parameters of an equation like (5-2). Even if this is not so, a linear model is often close enough over the relevant range to the shape of the curve usually encountered to serve for practical purposes. However, it is impossible to determine the exact type of effect the variables have, i.e., whether the variables studied affect learning rate or learning limit. It is important to note, however, that their work usually demonstrates a strong intuitive feeling for the fact that they are describing a learning process.[10]

A variant of (5-2) was used by Dernburg in his study of television.[11] Suppose the data is strictly cross-sectional in nature, and assume that (1) the rate of learning is a linear function of factors determining it, and (2) $\lambda = 1$. The value of t holding at the instant the data are taken may then be thought of as being absorbed into the coefficients, and the following equation may be written:

$$Y_t = \frac{1}{1 + \exp\left(a_1 - \sum_i b_i X_i\right)}.$$

This is a form of multivariate logistic distribution. If $\lambda \neq 1$, it is possible that use of this equation might give peculiar results.

9. See, for instance, J. H. Copp, "Toward Generalization in Farm Practice Research," *Rural Sociology*, vol. 23, no. 1, 1958, pp. 103ff.

10. This literature is reviewed in H. F. Lionberger, *Adoption of New Ideas and Practices*, Iowa State University Press, Amos, Iowa, 1960, and E. M. Rogers, *Diffusion of Innovations*, The Free Press, New York, 1962.

11. T. F. Dernburg, "Consumer Response to Innovation: Television," in *Studies in Household Economic Behavior*, Yale Studies in Economics, vol. 9, Yale University, New Haven, Connecticut, 1958.

Another source of potential trouble would be if the cross-section data represented numbers taken at different values of t. Examination of the results reported by Dernburg suggest that indeed $\lambda \neq 1$; it follows that the results obtained probably confuse the effects of factors on learning rate and on the long-run probability of a consumer's owning a television set.

Massy has also studied the innovations of television.[12] He considers an equation of the form of (3-17). Using time instead of trials, he assumes that

$$1 - \alpha = \prod_j Z_j^{a_0{}^j + a_1{}^j Y_n},$$

so that the resulting equation, where the Z_j's represent factors affecting the learning rate, is

$$\frac{dY_n}{dt} = X_0 \left(\prod^j Z_j^{a_0{}^j + a_1{}^j Y_n} \right) \lambda Y_n - \left(\prod^j Z_j^{a_0{}^j + a_1{}^j Y_n} \right) Y_n^2.$$

Massy identifies the Z_j's with product price and consumer income. Even though he does not assume $\lambda = 1$, it seems sensible to argue that these factors will surely affect the asymptotic probability of a consumer's owning a television set. In fact, Massy argues that the parameters he estimates (the $a_0{}^j$ and $a_1{}^j$) reflect elasticities of demand, although it is clear that they do not but rather reflect the influence of these factors upon the rate of consumer learning. Massy finds that the parameter values he obtains are not consistent with the notion that he is estimating elasticities of demand, which is really not surprising at all because they are not, in fact, estimates of demand elasticities.

Thus it becomes clear that reference to the basic model of behavior presented here is an aid to understanding previous work, and is also supported by previous empirical studies. It must also

12. W. F. Massy, *Innovation and Market Penetration*, Massachusetts Institute of Technology, Cambridge, Massachusetts: Ph.D. thesis, 1960.

be clear that the term *consumer* as used in this study refers to any consumer of products, not just individuals purchasing items in a supermarket, and that the basic theory appears to be relevant to all aspects of consumer behavior.

Measuring Preferences

Now that the general applicability of the model has been discussed, it is time to discuss how consumer preferences for products may be measured and what the value is of such measurement.

A classical method of measuring preferences is to give a number of people paired comparison tests. Each pair is compared by the subject, and the item of the pair that is preferred is indicated by the subject. The resulting data may then be analyzed according to a procedure suggested by Guilford to produce a scale.[13] The procedure is as follows. First, a matrix summarizing the preferences of individual is constructed. The number of rows and columns is equal to the total number of items being compared; each row or column represents one of the items. The preferences in the matrix are coded as a 1 if the row item is preferred to the column item. A zero is entered in the symmetrically opposite cell if, as is often done, the symmetrically opposite paired comparison test was not run. The matrices are then aggregated over all individuals. The elements of the aggregate matrix are then converted to proportions of individuals preferring any row entry to any column entry, summing over the rows proportions of preferences for each item. Finally, this average proportion is converted to a scale on a standard score basis, in which 0 is a neutral point indicating that the item is preferred one-half the time in comparison to all other items. Positive scale values indicate a higher proportion of preferences, negative a lower proportion.

13. J. P. Guilford, *Psychometric Methods*, 2nd ed., McGraw-Hill Book Company, New York, 1954, chap. 7.

There are two possible conceptual problems with this procedure. First, it implicitly assumes a scale can be constructed that is meaningful. Second, no measure of the ability of respondents to discriminate between alternatives is provided.[14]

The first problem requires some further explication. It is typically assumed that the scale results can be used *as if* a so-called "strong axiom of revealed preference" held, i.e., if there are n distinct alternatives (denoted $a^0, a^1, \ldots, a^n$), then $a^0 R a^1, a^1 R a^2, \ldots, a^{n-1} R a^n \Rightarrow \sim (a^n R a^0)$, where R means revealed preferred and $\sim$ denotes negation. In other words, if there are n alternatives such that a^i, the ith alternative, is preferred to a^{i+1} for $i = 0, 1, \ldots, n - 1$, then a^n cannot be revealed as preferred to a^0 if the strong axiom of revealed preferences holds.

This is the case that allows construction of a meaningful scale. If the condition of the strong axiom is not met, then it is not possible to infer backward from the scale the actual choices that would be observed.[15] The presence or absence of this condition, which might be called *the condition requisite for consistency of behavior*, may be readily tested.[16] The test may be briefly summarized. Let A be the aggregate matrix of proportions, derived according to the given rules. The first computation of the next step in the Guilford procedure is to compute a matrix $B = [b_{ij}] = [a_{ij} - a_{ii}]$. From B, derive a matrix C, where

$$C_{ij} = 1 \text{ if } b_{ij} \leq 0, i \neq j,$$

$$= 0 \text{ otherwise.}$$

14. This discussion omits the classic problems of validity and reliability that must, of course, be solved in any actual applied use of scaling procedures. For discussion of these problems, see Guilford, *op. cit.*

15. This situation does not imply that the measurement procedure is unreliable. It may, indeed, be extremely reliable.

16. A. R. Dobell, "A Comment on A. Y. C. Koo's 'An Empirical Test of Revealed Preference Theory'," *Econometrica*, vol. 33, no. 2, April, 1965. A second article that discusses the appropriate test is J. B. Kernan, "Paired Comparisons and Graph Theory," *Journal of Marketing Research*, vol. 4, no. 1, February, 1967.

A sufficient condition that the observations show a violation of the consistency requirement is that the matrix C not be nilpotent. One can test this simply by deleting an alternative associated with a zero row or zero column and by constructing the principal submatrix of C corresponding to the reduced set. This principal submatrix is then examined for zero rows or columns, and the process continued. If the entire set cannot be so deleted, the consistency is violated. Koo has presented a technique for determining the maximum size of the consistent subset in cases where inconsistency is found.[17]

This procedure allows a direct, but weak, test to be made of whether the conditions outlined in Chapter 1 for the inapplicability of the traditional theory of consumer behavior are met: If consumer preferences do not meet the consistency requirement, the traditional theory may not be applicable. The test is weak because a shift in preferences can clearly occur that will not violate the consistency requirement, given the aggregate nature of data that would commonly be used in the test.

The second problem, that of obtaining a measure of the ability of respondents to discriminate between alternatives, can be overcome only by replication. Kuehn and Day have given a method for estimating the discrimination ability of respondents.[18] This method will be briefly reviewed because of its relevance to how it was proposed to handle preference measurement in the model discussed in Chapters 2 and 3.

Kuehn and Day divide the range of consumer preferences with respect to the product characteristic under study into n segments. Associated with each segment $1, 2, \ldots, n$ is an unknown u_i, the proportion of consumers weighted by volume of the product they are likely to consume having a preference for the product-characteristic value specified by the segment i. Then let

17. A. Y. C. Koo, "An Empirical Test of Revealed Preference Theory," *Econometrica*, vol. 31, no. 3, October, 1963, pp. 646–664, and A. Y. C. Koo, "Reply," *Econometrica*, vol. 33, no. 2, April, 1965.
18. A. A. Kuehn and R. L. Day, "Strategy of Product Quality," *op. cit.*

p_{jk} be the probability that a consumer whose preference falls into the category specified by segment i would prefer a product brand with that characteristic to a brand with a product-characteristic value in segment k. In the aggregate, $p_{kj}{}^i$ then represents the probability that consumers in the ith category would choose a brand with characteristic k.

Finally, one has to take into account the consumers' ability to discriminate differences in product characteristics. Let d_c represent the consumers' ability to discriminate with respect to the product attribute in question. Then,

$$p_{jk}{}^i = \frac{(1 - d_c)^{|j - i|}}{(1 - d_c)^{|j-i|} + (1 - d_c)^{|k - i|}}. \qquad (5\text{-}4)$$

If consumers cannot discriminate between products with different values of the characteristic, $d_c = 0$; perfect discrimination implies $d_c = 1$. The parameters to be estimated are $w_i (i = 1, \ldots, n)$ and d_c. If the product has only one relevant characteristic, a simple modification of (5-4) represents the P'_i value of Chapter 3: the relative appeal of the product under consideration.

$$P'_i = \frac{(1 - d_c)^{|C_B - i|}}{\sum\limits_{B=1}^{k} (1 - d_c)^{|C_B - i|}}. \qquad (5\text{-}5)$$

where i denotes the relevant cell, C_B the brand's product characteristic value, and B an index summing over brands available. In order to convert this value to an overall one, it is necessary to combine the cells. If the specified w_i is known, this can be readily done: P' overall $= \Sigma w_i P'_i$. Similarly, if more than one characteristic is important, the effects of these may be put together if their relative importance is known.[19] The parameters in (5-4) may be

19. Alternatively, the analysis may be carried out on a cell-by-cell basis. See A. A. Kuehn and D. L. Weiss, "Marketing Analysis Training Exercise." In this case there is one equation (3-12) for each cell of the preference scale, and sales at any time are summed after being computed on a cell-by-cell basis. It may be noted that once again a ratio-scale utility measurement is being used.

estimated by using forced-choice paired-comparison tests. A single test gives an estimate of P_{jk} and therefore of P_{kj} since the two must add to one. The expected value of P_{jk} is simply

$$\mathscr{E}(P_{jk}) = \sum_{i=1}^{n} w_i P_{jk}{}^i.$$

Each single comparison test provides one equation. Further,

$$\sum_{i=1}^{n} w_i = 1.$$

Therefore, n single comparison tests allow the parameters w_i $(i = 1, 2, \ldots, n)$ and d_c to be estimated.[20]

The basic features of the problem and a proposed solution have now been outlined. This construction creates the possibility of predicting new-product success from product-characteristic measurements. It may be readily seen that if consumer preferences for a proposed new product are measured against existing products, it is then possible to project a predicted sales path from this information alone. Such analysis is partial in nature, neglecting competitive reaction and the sponsoring firm's own marketing efforts. These effects need not be ignored as they can be readily estimated also if some idea of sensible parameter values has already been obtained. Thus this model allows early prediction of whether a new product will be successful or not. Further, as the example presented in Chapter 4 illustrates, the model allows a very rapid determination of the success or failure of a new product to be made once the product is placed on the market.

---

20. One brand should be tested whose characteristics fall at each extreme ($i = 1$ and $i = n$) to establish the full range of consumer preferences. It can be seen that the actual solution process requires numerical analysis techniques.

The Relation Between This Model and Two Other Models of Consumer Behavior

The first two sections of this chapter have illustrated the general applicability of the model and discussed how the effect of product preferences of consumers might be measured and built into the model. The purpose of this section is to review the relation between the model that this book has discussed and two other probabilistic models of consumer behavior.

The Negative-Binomial-Distribution Model

The negative binomial distribution is a two-parameter distribution for the nonnegative integers $0, 1, 2, 3, 4, \ldots, r$. If the two parameters are taken as the mean m and the exponent k, the probability P_r of observing a number r is

$$P_r = \left(1 + \frac{m}{k}\right)^{-k} \frac{\Gamma(k + k - 1)}{\Gamma(r)(k - 1)} \left(\frac{m}{m + k}\right)^r.$$

This distribution has been employed by Ehrenberg and others as a means of ordering consumer-panel data.[21] Ehrenberg suggests that it is often convenient to use instead of k the parameter $a = m/k$. Using the negative binomial distribution implies basically a two-dimensional model. The dimensions are similar to those already discussed, one dimension being time and the other, an unordered one, consumers. If, in fact, one can assume that the purchases of any particular consumer in successive periods of time behave like independent random samples from a Poisson distribution and that consumers follow a χ^2 distribution, then the negative binomial distribution will fit purchase

21. References to their work are A. S. C. Ehrenberg, "The Pattern of Consumer Purchases," *Applied Statistics*, vol. 8, 1959, pp. 26–41, and A. S. C. Ehrenberg, C. Chatfield, and G. J. Goodhart, "Progress on a Simplified Model of Stationary Purchasing Behavior," *Journal of the Royal Statistical Society*, vol. 129, 1966, pp. 317–367.

data aggregated over consumers. Such assumptions, of course, are essentially barren in a behavioral sense; the Ehrenberg approach is an example of fitting data to a reasonable probability distribution. The next goal is to attempt to assign meaning to the results. To do this, it is sensible to present first a brief review of what the results look like.

The negative binomial distribution is always positively skewed. It has one mode, which is at zero for the fairly small values of m and k that occur with consumer purchasing data, so that the distribution is then a reversed J shape. Chapter 4, in the section on method-of-moments estimation, showed that this shape of distribution should arise and be fitted quite nicely with respect to purchase occasions but not quantities, the measure of consumer response Ehrenberg has used. In fact, Ehrenberg does report that systematic biases appear that indicate the negative binomial distribution is not a completely adequate fit.

If the preceding anlysis is correct, the use of purchase occasions over a predecided time span rather than purchase quantities should noticeably improve the fit of the negative binomial model. This question has been investigated by Grahn using the same data used in Chapter 4.[22] The results obtained are precisely what would be expected given the stated predictions. First, "the NBD as employed by Ehrenberg did not fit the data."[23] When the proper data are employed (e.g., purchase occasions), the NBD fits in the sense that, using a χ^2 test, there is no significant difference between the observed and predicted, or theoretical, distributions. To summarize, if the theory developed previously is correct, then it is predicted that a modified NBD will fit the data. The prediction is confirmed.[24]

22. Gary L. Grahn, "The Negative Binomial Distribution Model of Repeat-Purchase Loyalty: An Empirical Investigation," Working Paper, Corporate Marketing Research, Owens-Illinois Corp., Toledo, Ohio.

23. *Ibid.*

24. It is useful to recall that in Chapter 4 in the section on minimum χ^2 estimation it was shown the data fit the theory.

The Response-Uncertainty Model

The response-uncertainty model, based on a latent Markov model, was proposed by James Coleman as a means of distinguishing real change from apparent change, or response uncertainty.[25] By *change* is meant a systematic, genuine shift in a person's state, such that an individual is in a state different from his original state. Movement in the responses of an individual reflect a genuine shift from the individual's original position. Response uncertainty means that any apparent shift in a person's state is not due to change but rather to the fact that an individual has responded differently without any underlying alteration of his state.

The distinction can be made clearer by use of an example given by Coleman. Suppose a survey were conducted in which people were asked if they were in favor of abolishing capital punishment. Forty-five per cent respond "Yes." A pure change model would assert that 45 per cent of those interviewed believe capital punishment should be abolished. A pure response-uncertainty model would say that any person will respond "Yes" 45 per cent of the time to the question, when he actually "doesn't know," or "has no opinion." It can be expected not to "fit" the previous data, for it has been already demonstrated that a model of change, in the sense of a consumer's learning about a new product, appears to be an appropriate one.

Before examining this question, a brief review of Coleman's model may be presented. Coleman begins by saying that rather than an individual as a unit undergoing change, it is the individual's set of response elements that determines if change occurs. The unit of change, then, is the response element, and each element is associated with a certain response. Thus the probability of giving response i is expressed as

$$P_i = \frac{m_i}{\sum\limits_{j=1}^{s} m_j},$$

25. James S. Coleman, *Models of Change and Response Uncertainty,* Prentice-Hall, Inc., Englewood Cliffs, New Jersey, 1964.

where m_i is response element i and S is the total number of responses. Coleman presents no behavioral interpretation of what he calls a *response element*. However, it is quite clear that this is actually ratio-scale utility measurement once again. Thus the Coleman and Kuehn models assume precisely the same thing about the long-run behavior of consumers. They differ, however, in two other aspects: First, the predicted equations for change are different, and, second, unlike Kuehn's there is nothing in the Coleman model to indicate what or how underlying factors affect P_i. To reiterate, however, it is clear that if Kuehn's learning model fits a set of data, it should be expected that response uncertainty (i.e., no learning) would not be found to explain the observed data. If v_{it} is the probability of an element being in state i at time t, then for a set of S states of an element,

$$\frac{dV_{it}}{dt} = q_{1i}V_{1t} + \cdots + q_{ii}V_{it} + \cdots + q_{Si}V_{St} \qquad i = 1, \ldots, S,$$

where q_{ij} is the transition rate for the element between state i and state j. This set of equations may be solved (noting that the probabilities involved sum to 1), yielding

$$V_{it} = V_{10}r_{1it} + V_{20}r_{2it} + \cdots + V_{S0}r_{Sit} \qquad i = 1, \ldots, S,$$

where r_{ijt} is the transition probability of change from state i to state j in the time period 0 to t.

The next step is to aggregate over individuals. The expected frequency of individuals at position V_i at time t is $V_iF(V_i, t)$ where $F(V_i, t)$ denotes the marginal distribution of individuals with respect to V_i. By aggregating this expression over all values of V_i, the expected proportion of individuals who give response i at time t is

$$P_{it} = \int_0^1 V_iF(V_i, t)\, dV_i.$$

By substitution, using the earlier formulae for V_{it}, this expected portion can be expressed in terms of r_{ijt}'s as

$$P_{i,t} = P_{10}r_{1it} + \cdots + P_{i0}r_{iit} + \cdots + P_{S0}r_{Sit}.$$

The basic problem is to obtain a measure of response uncertainty in terms of purchase at time 0. To obtain these estimates, it is necessary to calculate response uncertainty over a period of time. These estimates, which are simply the expected proportion of those who give response i at time 0 and response j at time t, are then used in the calculation of the response uncertainty at time 0. If, for example, the data are values at time 0 and time 2 and there are S states in the system, then the expected proportion of people giving response i at time 0 and response j at time 2 would be P_{i0j2}.

$$P_{i0j2} = \sum_{k=1}^{S} P_{i0k1}r_{kjt} \qquad (i = 1, \ldots, S).$$

This can be more clearly written in matrix form as

$$P_{SxS}(0, 2) = P_{SxS}(0, 1)R_{SxS}(t),$$

which implies

$$P(0, 1)^{-1}P(0, 2) = R(t).$$

Thus the transition probabilities r_{ij} at time t may be readily calculated from estimates of P_{i0j1} and P_{i0j2}. The equilibrium distribution of all individuals who give response i at time t can then readily be found. The equation is

$$P_{ie} = P_{ie}r_{1it} + \cdots + P_{ie}r_{iit} + \cdots + R_{Se}r_{Sit},$$

where P_{ie} is the expected proportion of individuals giving response i at equilibrium.

It is also possible to develop a measure of the net change in individuals, ΔC_{it}, with respect to a given dimension i.

$$\Delta C_{it} = P_{11}r_{1it} + \cdots + P_{i1}(r_{iit} - 1) + \cdots + P_{S1}r_{Sit}$$
$$= P_{i2} - P_{i1},$$

where the P's are the expected proportions of individuals giving response i at some given time.

Finally, the transition rates q_{ij} may be estimated by an iterative process applied to an infinite series.

$$q_{ij} = r_{ijt} - \frac{t^2}{2!} \sum_{k=1}^{S} q_{ik}q_{kj} - \frac{t^3}{3!} \sum_{k=1}^{S} \sum_{h=1}^{S} q_{ik}q_{kh}q_{kj} - \cdots.$$

At time 0, all q_{ij}'s are taken to be zero, so that at time 1, q_{ij} is estimated by r_{ijt}. Thus a start can be made; the iteration continues until the last term in the series is beyond some threshold of accuracy.

The analysis has now proceeded to the point where it is possible to present the method Coleman proposes to measure response uncertainty. Note that values of r_{ijt} and q_{ij} can be computed according to the preceding equations, given data.

Let time t represent the time from observation 1 to observation 2, and time T the time from observation 0 to observation 1. From the values of r_{ijt} and q_{ij}, estimates of the expected proportion giving response i at time 0 and response j at time 1 and of the expected proportion giving response i at time 0 and response j at time 2 may be calculated as P_{i0j} and P_{i0j2}, respectively. The values r_{ijt} are coefficients that translate a response at time 1 to a corresponding response at time 2. Thus,

$$P_{i0j2} = \sum_{k=1}^{S} P_{i0k0}r_{kjT}.$$

If the values of r_{ijT} were known, then the relation

$$P_{i0j1} = \sum_{k=1}^{S} P_{i0k0} r_{kjT}$$

could be solved for the P_{i0k0}'s, and response uncertainty at time 0 could be estimated. To do this, Coleman assumes the q_{ij}'s are exactly the same for time 0 to time 1 as for time 1 to time 2. Then the problem is solved; if the time between 0 and 1 is equal to the time between 1 and 2, then $r_{ijT} = r_{ijt}$. In a similar fashion, values for response uncertainty at times 1 and 2 can be found. The values of the response uncertainties should be positive; if they turn out negative, this is evidence that the model does not fit and is not useful.[26]

James Ming has examined the question of whether the Coleman model fits using the data used in Chapter 4.[27] He finds that the data and the model do not fit well, as evidenced by many negative values of response uncertainty. This is not a surprising result; if learning is taking place, and the evidence suggests it is, then a model of response uncertainty should not fit well at all. However, this model and approach could well be of value in evaluating consumer behavior during periods of stable preferences when change is not occurring.

Recapitulation

At this point a reconsideration of the fundamental argument presented in this book will be briefly given. The initial chapter

26. This is a somewhat inexact test. Montgomery has proposed some other tests and extended the Coleman model in David B. Montgomery, "A Probability Diffusion Model of Dynamic Market Behavior," Working Paper 205-66, Alfred P. Sloan School of Business, Massachusetts Institute of Technology, Cambridge, Massachusetts, May, 1966.

27. James H. Ming, "An Analysis, Interpretation, and Evaluation of a Model of Change and Response Uncertainty When Applied to Consumer Purchase Behavior," Working Paper, May, 1967.

showed that there are certain situations where traditional demand analysis is not entirely sufficient. These situations were characterized as arising from a shift in consumer preferences that also alters the substitution relationships between commodities. A brief overview of a learning model of consumer behavior was presented as a means of coping with the problem, and it was pointed out that in the long run the learning model might not differ in substance from traditional demand analysis.

The next chapter reviewed in detail learning models of consumer behavior. This chapter argued that the behavioral assumptions underlying a learning model should be similar to those underlying demand analysis and showed that this was not true of the first-order Markov chain with brands purchased as states. The chapter concluded by stating the aggregation problem inherent in the simplest model that has an appropriate behavioral basis.

The third chapter reviewed some proposed solutions to the aggregation problem and presented simple extensions of the model. Next a detailed discussion of estimation- and hypothesis-testing procedures for the subject-controlled learning model was presented. Three appendices covering computational details and computer programs were also presented. The intention here was to make every effort to provide the reader with the capability for repeating the analysis in the chapter and performing his own analysis.

Finally, this chapter has shown how to apply the model to durable goods, how to measure consumer preferences, and how the learning model central to this book relates to two other models of consumer behavior.

Concluding Comments

This concludes the discussion of the new theory of consumer behavior. It can be seen that the surface has been scratched. In particular, use of the theory presented in this text would enable an individual company to make optimal allocations on advertising, distribution pricing, and product policy; or, alternatively, the model could be turned around and converted into a model of oligopoly behavior—if the classical and hoary problem of defining an industry (or branch of a utility tree) could be solved. This conclusion is really a beginning.

Bibliography

1. ALCHIAN, A., "Uncertainty, Evolution, and Economic Theory," *Journal of Political Economy*, vol. 60, no. 1, June, 1950, pp. 211–221.
2. ALLVINE, F. C., *The Patronage Decision-Making Process*, Indiana University, Bloomington, Indiana: DBA thesis, 1966.
3. ANSCOMBE, F. J., "Estimating a Mixed Exponential Response Law," *Journal of the American Statistical Association*, vol. 56, September, 1961, pp. 493–502.
4. ATKINSON, R. C., G. H. BOWER, and E. J. CROTHERS, *An Introduction to Mathematical Learning Theory*, John Wiley & Sons, Inc., New York, 1965.
5. BASMANN, R. L., *Application of Several Econometric Techniques to a Theory of Demand with Variable Tastes*, Iowa State College, Ames, Iowa: Ph.D. thesis, 1955.
6. ———, "A Note on an Invariant Property of Shifts in Demand," *Metroeconomica*, vol. 6, no. 2, 1954.
7. ———, "A Theory of Demand with Variable Consumer Preferences," *Econometrica*, vol. 24, no. 1, 1956, pp. 47–58.
8. BENJAMIN, B., W. P. JOLLY, and J. MAITLAND, "Operational Research and Advertising: Theories of Response," *Operational Research Quarterly*, vol. 11, no. 4, December, 1960.

9. BUSH, R. R., and MOSTELLER, F., *Stochastic Models for Learning*, John Wiley & Sons, Inc., New York, 1955.

10. CARMAN, J. M., "Brand Switching and Linear Learning Models," *Journal of Advertising Research*, vol. 6, no. 2, June, 1966, pp. 23–31.

11. ———, "Brand Switching and Linear Learning Models: Some Empirical Results," Working Paper no. 20, Research Program in Marketing, Graduate School of Business Administration, University of California, Berkeley, California, August 6, 1965.

12. CARTWRIGHT, D., and A. ZANDER, *Group Dynamics*, 2nd ed., Harper & Row, Publishers, New York, 1960.

13. CLARKSON, G. P. E., *Portfolio Selection: A Simulation of Trust Investment*, Prentice-Hall, Inc., Englewood Cliffs, New Jersey, 1962.

14. ———, "Verification and the Function of Laws in Microeconomics," *Industrial Management Review*, vol. 4, no. 1, 1962, pp. 41–58.

15. COLEMAN, J. S., *Models of Change and Response Uncertainty*, Prentice-Hall, Inc., Englewood Cliffs, New Jersey, 1964.

16. COPP, J. H., "Toward Generalization in Farm Practice Research," *Rural Sociology*, vol. 23, no. 1, 1958.

17. CRAMER, H., *Mathematical Methods of Statistics*, Princeton University Press, Princeton, New Jersey, 1958.

18. DAY, R. L., *Marketing Models*, International Textbook Company, Scranton, Pennsylvania, 1964.

19. DERNBURG, T. F., "Consumer Response to Innovation: Television," in *Studies in Household Economic Behavior*, Yale Studies in Economics, vol. 9, Yale University, New Haven, Connecticut, 1958.

20. DOBELL, A. R., "A Comment on A. Y. C. Koo's 'An Empirical Test of Revealed Preference Theory,'" *Econometrica*, vol. 33, no. 2, April, 1965.

21. DUESENBERRY, J. S., *Income, Saving and the Theory of Consumer Behavior*, Harvard University Press, Cambridge, Massachusetts, 1949.

22. EHRENBERG, A. S. C., "An Appraisal of Markov Brand-Switching Models," *Journal of Marketing Research*, vol. 2, no. 4, November, 1965.

23. ———, "The Pattern of Consumer Purchases," *Applied Statistics*, vol. 8, 1959.

24. ———, C. CHATFIELD, and G. J. GOODHART, "Progress on a Simplified Model of Stationary Purchasing Behavior," *Journal of the Royal Statistical Society*, vol. 129, 1966.

25. ESTES, W. K., *et al.*, *Modern Learning Theory*, Appleton-Century-Crofts, New York, 1954.

26. FEIGENBAUM, E. A., and J. FELDMAN, eds., *Computers and Thought*, McGraw-Hill Book Company, New York, 1963.

27. FELDMAN, J., "Computer Simulation of Cognitive Processes," in H. Borko, ed., *Computer Applications in the Behavioral Sciences*, Prentice-Hall, Inc., Englewood Cliffs, New Jersey, 1962, chap. 15.

28. FELLNER, W., "Does the Market Direct the Relative Factor-Saving Effects of Technological Progress?" in *The Rate and Direction of Inventive Activity: Economic and Social Factors*, Princeton University Press, Princeton, New Jersey, 1962.

29. FOURT, L. A., and J. W. WOODLOCK, "Early Prediction of Market Success for New Grocery Products," *Journal of Marketing*, vol. 26, no. 2, October, 1960.

30. FRANK, R., "Brand Choice as a Probability Process," *Journal of Business*, vol. 35, no. 1, January, 1962.

31. GIRSHICK, M. A., F. MOSTELLER, and L. J. SAVAGE, "Unbiased Estimates for Certain Binomial Sampling Problems with Applications," *Annals of Mathematical Statistics*, vol. 17, 1946, pp. 13–23.

32. GOLDBERG, S., *Introduction to Difference Equations*, John Wiley & Sons, Inc., New York, 1958.

33. GRAHN, G. L., "The Negative Binomial Distribution Model of Repeat Purchase Loyalty," Working Paper, Corporate Marketing Research, Owen-Illinois Corp., Toledo, Ohio.

34. GRILICHES, Z., "Hybrid Corn," *Econometrica*, vol. 25, no. 4, October, 1957.

35. GUILFORD, J. P., *Psychometric Methods*, 2nd ed., McGraw-Hill Book Company, New York, 1954.

36. HAINES, G. H., JR., "A Theory of Market Behavior After Innovation," *Management Science*, vol. 10, no. 4, July, 1964, pp. 634–658.

37. HARARY, F., and B. LIPSTEIN, "The Dynamics of Brand Loyalty: A Markovian Approach," *Operations Research*, vol. 10, no. 1, January–February, 1962.

38. HERNITER, J. D., "Stochastic Market Models and the Analysis of Consumer Panel Data," in *American Chemical Society (Division of Chemical Marketing and Economics), Symposia on General Rubber Chemicals and Marketing Economics Purchase and Exchange of Technical Know-How Mathematical Models in Chemical Marketing*, American Chemical Society, New York, 1966.

39. ———, and R. A. HOWARD, "Stochastic Marketing Models," in *Progress in Operations Research*, vol. 2, John Wiley & Sons, Inc., New York, 1963.

40. HILGARD, E. R., *Introduction to Psychology*, 2nd ed., Harcourt, Brace & World, Inc., New York, 1957.

41. ———, *Theories of Learning*, Appleton-Century-Crofts, New York, 1956.

42. HUFF, D. L., *Determination of Intraurban Retail Trade Areas*, Real Estate Research Program, University of California, Los Angeles, 1962.

43. HULL, C. L., *Principles of Behavior: An Introduction to Behavior Theory*, Appleton-Century-Crofts, New York, 1943.

44. HUNT, E. B., *Concept Formation: An Information Processing Problem*, John Wiley & Sons, Inc., New York, 1962.

45. ICHIMURA, S., "A Critical Note on the Definition of Related Goods," *Review of Economic Studies*, vol. 18, 1950–1951, pp. 179–183.

46. KELLY, R. F., "The Diffusion Model as a Predictor of Ultimate Patronage Levels in New Retail Outlets," in R. M. Haas, ed., *Science, Technology, and Marketing*, American Marketing Association, Chicago, Illinois, 1967.

47. KERNAN, J. B., "Paired Comparisons and Graph Theory," *Journal of Marketing Research*, vol. 4, no. 1, February, 1967.

48. KOO, A. Y. C., "An Empirical Test of Revealed Preference Theory," *Econometrica*, vol. 31, no. 3, October, 1963.

49. ———, "Reply," *Econometrica*, vol. 33, no. 2, April, 1965.

50. KUEHN, A. A., *An Analysis of the Dynamics of Consumer Behavior and Its Implications for Marketing Management*, Carnegie Institute of Technology, Pittsburgh, Pennsylvania: Ph.D. thesis, 1958.

51. ———, "Mathematical Models of Consumer Behavior," in J. W. Newman, ed., *On Knowing the Consumer*, John Wiley & Sons, Inc., New York, 1966.

52. ———, "A Model for Budgeting Advertising," in F. M. Bass et al., eds., *Mathematical Models and Methods in Marketing*, Richard D. Irwin, Inc., Homewood, Illinois, 1961.

53. ———, and R. L. DAY, "Strategy of Product Quality," *Harvard Business Review*, vol. 40, November–December, 1962, pp. 100–110.

54. ———, and D. L. WEISS, "Marketing Analysis Training Exercise," *Behavioral Science*, vol. 10, no. 1, January, 1965, pp. 51–67.

55. ———, T. W. MCGUIRE, and D. L. WEISS, "Measuring the Effectiveness of Advertising," in R. M. Haas, ed., *Science, Technology, and Marketing*, American Marketing Association, Chicago, Illinois, January, 1967.

56. LANCASTER, K. J., "A New Approach to Consumer Theory," *Journal of Political Economy*, vol. 74, no. 2, April, 1966.

57. LAWRENCE, R. J., "Models of Consumer Purchasing Behavior," *Applied Statistics*, vol. 15, no. 3, November, 1966, pp. 216–233.
58. LIONBERGER, H. F., *Adoption of New Ideas and Practices*, Iowa State University Press, Ames, Iowa, 1960.
59. LONGTON, P. A., and B. T. WARNER, "A Mathematical Model for Marketing," *Metra*, vol. 1, no. 3, September, 1962.
60. LUCE, R. D., *Individual Choice Behavior*, John Wiley & Sons, Inc., New York, 1959.
61. MAFFEI, R. B., "Brand Preferences and Simple Markov Processes," *Operations Research*, vol. 8, no. 2, March–April, 1960, pp. 210–218.
62. MANSFIELD, E., "Comment," in *The Rate and Direction of Inventive Activity: Economic and Social Factors*, Princeton University Press, Princeton, New Jersey, 1962.
63. ———, "Intrafirm Rates of Diffusion of an Innovation," *The Review of Economics and Statistics*, vol. 45, no. 4, November, 1963.
64. ———, "Technological Change and the Rate of Imitation," *Econometrica*, vol. 29, no. 4, October, 1961.
65. MARTIN, H., and E. REISSNER, *Elementary Differential Equations*, Addison-Wesley, Reading, Massachusetts, 1956.
66. MASSY, W. F., "Estimation of Parameters for Linear Learning Models," Working Paper no. 78, Graduate School of Business, Stanford University, Palo Alto, California, October, 1965.
67. ———, *Innovation and Market Penetration*, Massachusetts Institute of Technology, Cambridge, Massachusetts: Ph.D. thesis, 1960.
68. ———, "Order and Homogeneity of Family Specific Brand-Switching Processes," *Journal of Marketing Research*, vol. 3, no. 1, February, 1966.
69. MING, J. H., "An Analysis, Interpretation, and Evaluation of a Model of Change and Response Uncertainty When Applied to Consumer Purchase Behavior," Working Paper, May, 1967.
70. MONTGOMERY, D. B., "A Probability Diffusion Model of Dynamic Market Behavior," Working Paper 205–66, Alfred P. Sloan School of Business, Massachusetts Institute of Technology, Cambridge, Massachusetts, May, 1966.
71. ———, "Stochastic Modeling of the Consumer," *Industrial Management Review*, vol. 8, no. 2, Spring, 1967.
72. OSTLE, B. F., *Statistics in Research*, Iowa State University Press, Ames, Iowa, 1954.
73. PEARL, H. S., and L. J. REED, "On the Mathematical Theory of Population Growth," *Metron*, vol. 3, no. 1, 1923.

74. ROBINSON, D. E., "The Economics of Fashion Demand," *Quarterly Journal of Economics*, vol. 75, no. 3, August, 1961.

75. ROGERS, E. M., *Diffusion of Innovations*, The Free Press, New York, 1962.

76. SCHUMPETER, J. A., *The Theory of Economic Development*, Harvard University Press, Cambridge, Massachusetts, 1934.

77. SILK, A. J., and S. MILLER, "Changes in Market Share and Advertising Strategy: A Re-examination," Graduate School of Business Administration, UCLA, Los Angeles, California: mimeographed manuscript, August, 1965.

78. SIMON, H. A., *Models of Man*, John Wiley & Sons, Inc., New York, 1957.

79. SUDMAN, S., "On the Accuracy of Recording of Consumer Panels: I and II," *Journal of Marketing Research*, vol. 1, nos. 2 and 3, respectively.

80. SUPPES, P., "Behavioristic Foundations of Utility," *Econometrica*, vol. 29, no. 2, April, 1961.

81. THEIL, H., "The Information Approach to Demand Analysis," *Econometrica*, vol. 33, no. 1, 1965, pp. 67–87.

82. TINTNER, G., "Complementarity and Shifts in Demand," *Metroeconomica*, vol. 4, no. 1, 1952, pp. 1–4.

83. ——, *Econometrics*, John Wiley & Sons, Inc., New York, 1952.

84. UDELL, J. G., "Prepurchase Behavior of Buyers of Small Electrical Appliances," *Journal of Marketing*, vol. 30, no. 4, October, 1966.

85. WALD, H., with L. JUREEN, *Demand Analysis*, John Wiley & Sons, Inc., New York, 1958.

86. YANCE, J. V., *Investment Behavior in the Railroad Industry*, Harvard University, Cambridge, Massachusetts: Ph.D. thesis, 1955.

87. ——, "Technological Change as a Learning Process," unpublished paper, no date.

Index